The Critical Poem

The Critical Poem

Borges, Paz, and Other Language-Centered Poets in Latin America

Thorpe Running

Lewisburg
Bucknell University Press
London: Associated University Presses

Associated University Presses
440 Forsgate Drive
Cranbury, NJ 08512

Associated University Presses
16 Barter Street
London WC1A 2AH, England

Associated University Presses
P.O. Box 338, Port Credit
Mississauga, Ontario
Canada L5G 4L8

The paper used in this publication meets the requirements
of the American National Standard for Permanence of Paper
for Printed Library Materials Z39.48-1984.

Library of Congress Cataloging-in-Publication Data

Running, Thorpe.
    The critical poem : Borges, Paz, and other language-centered poets
in Latin America / Thorpe Running.
        p.   cm.
    Includes bibliographical references (p.   ) and index.
    ISBN 0-8387-5319-1 (alk. paper)
    1. Spanish American poetry—20th century—History and criticism.
2. Poetics.   I. Title.
PQ7082.P7R86   1996
861—dc20   95-45747
                                                                 CIP

PRINTED IN THE UNITED STATES OF AMERICA

For the Bensons

Contents

Introduction

THE eight poets studied in this book—Octavio Paz and David Huerta from Mexico; Roberto Juarroz, Jorge Luis Borges, Alejandra Pizarnik, and Alberto Girri from Argentina; Juan Luis Martínez and Gonzalo Millán from Chile—all share a deep fascination with what lies behind words in poems. A skeptical attitude toward language leads all eight to write what Octavio Paz has called "critical poetry," a poetry that questions its own construction.

In its own way, this body of philosophical poetic texts is as groundbreaking as were the novels of the well-known "Boom" in Latin American literature of the 1960s and 1970s. Those novels attracted a wide readership in many languages. Gabriel García Márquez's *One Hundred Years of Solitude,* for example, was on the best-seller list in several countries for many months in the late 1960s. Poets, however—even the more popular or accessible ones—have not had such good fortune, but a lack of wide readership is something they are resigned to from the outset. The poets included in this study have, for the most part, created additional obstacles for their readers, since they write poems that deal with their own construction and move toward a philosophy of language.

What gives these authors the drive and energy to write poetry that examines the very foundations of literature, when they know their audience is going to be limited? I have raised this topic with some of these poets. At first they may laugh, since they know how underappreciated their work is. Then they tend to muse about how living for poetry is something they just need to do. But at the same time they cannot hide the intensity with which they approach their writing. Roberto Juarroz could be speaking for them all when he articulates a view of the poet as having an essential, even ethical purpose. For Juarroz, this means that the only true poets are those who commit themselves to a "thinking" poetry; who take seriously their relationship with the words they use. All the poets in this study fall within Juarroz's definition. They share a commitment to a poetry of intellectual exploration, especially in the realm of language and its problems, and are not the first Spanish-language poets to address this topic in their poetry, as the initial chapter will explain. But they are the only constellation of poets—writing within the same general time frame (the 1960s through the 1980s) and the same geographical area—to have language as an urgent metapoetic concern.

My interest in poetry about poetry—that is, poetry *critical* of poetry—began after reading Roberto Juarroz's *Poesía vertical* in the early 1980s. Juarroz, obviously pushing the limits of poetic expression, indeed questioning the very possibility of saying *anything* in a poem, was clearly going in a new direction. Immediately I saw connections between Juarroz's explorative verse and the work of Octavio Paz, as well as fascinating parallels between this new kind of probing poetry and the writing of various poststructuralist critics—especially this notion that language is an untrustworthy tool and that literary texts contain elements that contradict their apparent structures. It soon became evident that other Latin American poets were developing an equally suspicious attitude toward words at work.

After working on this project for some time, I realized I would need to look for the poetics that lay behind this poetry about words that don't work. That poetics, however, could only be established after working through the poetry of the various writers who were mining this fruitful, if seemingly disheartening, vein. Finally, as Andrew Debicki reminded me, I would have to show what kind of texts were actually being written by these writers who professed such a profound distrust of language. Could they provide an answer for the contemporary poet beset by the crisis of language? As I worked on this topic, I published essays on a number of poets. Some of those articles, published in *Revista Iberoamericana, Chasqui, Alba de América,* and *Revista de Occidente,* provided a basis for several chapters. An early version of chapter 7 appeared in *Borges the Poet,* edited by Carlos Cortínez (Fayetteville: Arkansas University Press, 1986).

I have worked on several of these chapters during three different summer seminars sponsored by the National Endowment for the Humanities. I am enormously indebted to the directors of those sessions—François Rigolot, Andrew Debicki, and Enrico Mario Santí—for their insightful comments, timely intellectual prodding, and continuing encouragement. I would also like to thank my colleagues at Saint John's University and the College of Saint Benedict, especially Sister Eva Hooker for her support of scholarly work, Father Mark Thamert for his help with some knotty problems, Ned Dubin for his lively explications of Mallarmé, Ray Larson for his prose scalpel, and Violeta Pintado for her intelligent reading of several of these chapters. I thank my wife, Cheryl, and daughters, Sara and Maren, for everything they do.

1

The Critical Poem

POETRY that is self-conscious about saying what it means and meaning what it says is not a completely new phenomenon. But recently in Latin America a poetry has emerged that expresses utter despair at not being able to say anything at all. The first writer to center some of his poetry around the idea of language in crisis was Octavio Paz. Paz avoids the despair that often accompanies this topic, perhaps in part because he devotes a fairly small number of pages from his many books specifically to the problem of language. In fact, he is able to write almost glibly, despite claiming a major distrust of language. In the next chapter I will show how, beginning with his earliest poems in the 1930s, Paz clearly expresses doubts about words being able to work, a concern that reappears throughout his subsequent poems and essays. Before looking at Paz's poetry, I would like to look at one of his particularly incisive essays as a way of providing a context for the phenomenon of a poetry centered on language that has sprung up in Latin America.

The three-paragraph essay, titled "What Does Poetry Name?," from *Corriente alterna* (1967) (published in English as *Alternating Current*),[1] sums up brilliantly, if almost too economically, what Paz sees as the underlying concern for the contemporary writer. In attempting to sum up the history of poetry in this brief piece, Paz specifically separates modern from "classical" verse. The primary division point for Paz is the "poetic *consciousness*" that developed with the Romantics and that lays the groundwork for the even greater self-awareness of the most recent poets. The second, and related, difference is in the type of "difficulty" in such poets as Góngora and Donne, as compared with Rimbaud and Mallarmé—with special emphasis on Góngora and Mallarmé as exemplars of the two traditions. Góngora's difficulties "are external: they are grammatical, linguistic, mythological." And Paz wittily observes that "Góngora is not obscure: he is complicated." In contrast, the

13

poetry of Rimbaud and Mallarmé is conceptually difficult to comprehend. These two, especially Mallarmé—whom he singles out in other essays as "opening up" modern writing—represent the beginning of modern poetry, which "is inseparable from the criticism of language."

Scattered throughout Paz's little essay are several sentences that are far-reaching, in spite of their extreme succinctness. Since Paz packs so much insight into these sentences, I would like to isolate and comment on the most important of them. Here is the first: "The poem does not refer to anything outside itself; what a word refers to is another word." This does not really describe modern poetry in general. For most modern poets, the language of their texts has a more or less mimetic function: to some extent, at least, it attempts to represent the world. Instead, Paz looks ahead to what he will call the critical poem, one that questions its own language.

Although a few recent critics specifically study the "idea of language" in modern poetry, they do not suggest that the poets they study are intending to question language's capacity to transmit a meaning. A good example is Gerald Bruns; in his *Modern Poetry and the Idea of Language,* he sees language as either functional (Orphic) or "poetic" (hermetic), the latter being a stronger concern for form or "stylistic effects" than for representing an idea.[2] This division would almost seem to put the modern poet in the same general category as the one Góngora occupies in Paz's essay— poets whose poetic effects come primarily from linguistic or formal elements. Jonathan Mayhew, in the introduction to his *Claudio Rodríguez and the Language of Poetic Vision,* expands on Bruns's categories, explaining these differences as those between the "motivated sign" (Cratylism)—where language imitates the world—and a belief in the "arbitrariness" of a language severed from the world, "making it a radically autonomous, 'hermetic' form of discourse."[3] Then Mayhew says, "The modern poet does not choose between motivation and arbitrariness but rather strives to construct a language that is at once expressive and autonomous." For Mayhew, therefore, the modern poet views language as either a faithful reflector of the world or a faithful creator of a self-contained discourse or both. Mayhew further sees this poetic language (for the modern poet) as self-conscious: aware of an "unmasking" function—the "capacity to see beyond the arbitrary signs of the world and thus to reveal the truth"—and also able to create a "new and more authentic speech."

I agree with Mayhew on all of those points with reference to modern poetry in general and to the generation of Claudio

Rodríguez in contemporary Spain in particular. The Paz essay carries us considerably farther, however. Although Octavio Paz is ostensibly referring to modern poetry in general in his essay, he is really calling up an even more self-conscious type of poetry, containing a highly critical view of language, of which his own would be a clear prototype: a more introspective text that does not "refer to anything outside itself." This concept is explained in the following sentence extracted from the same essay: "The meaning does not reside outside the poem but within it, not in what the words say, but in *what they say to each other.*"

Surprisingly, given the extreme succinctness of this whole essay, the first part of this sentence seems almost redundant. But it reaffirms and emphasizes the modern poem's lack of external reference, as well as asserting that its significance lies *within* the text. How this happens depends on a distinction made about language: between what "words say" and what "*they say to each other*" (this is Paz's emphasis, felicitously). On one level we can take this distinction to be much the same one that Bruns and Mayhew make, respectively, between the motivated sign (or Orphic language) and arbitrary language (hermetic poetry). In the former, language refers to, or represents, the world (where words "say"). With arbitrary or hermetic language the text forms its own meaning, and this enclosed structure depends on words' relationship, on what they "say," to each other.

There is even more to Paz's statement, however. For one thing, it destroys completely any legitimacy for the "New Criticism's" claim of being able to give a single, best reading for any text. At the very least, Paz's sentence would support Michael Riffaterre's definition of a poem as "a text which says one thing and means another."[4] To go even further, this statement gives credence to the idea of the "open" text, one that allows multiple readings. For if all the words are interacting with each other, this implies an infinite number of possible permutations of the text. Paz also seems to be pointing presciently to the validity, if not necessity, of giving each poem a semiotic reading—that is, seeing how the words' various meanings (their "semantic fields") tie together on different levels and in different contexts.

Finally, this process of words' "saying to each other" edges toward a preview of poststructuralist views of language, especially the idea of language being a "differential network of meaning," as we will see shortly. In addition, as Paz goes back almost a century to find the precursors of the modern poem, he will point out elements of their poetry that can also be seen as coinciding remarkably well with poststructuralist ideas, as in this sentence from his essay: "In Rimbaud and Mallarmé language turns back upon itself, it ceases to designate, it is neither a symbol of, nor does it refer to, external realities, whether physical or suprasensible objects." Again, the idea of language turning "back upon itself" looks like another example of "hermetic" poetry. Rimbaud's is especially hermetic, and Paz says that in his works "the attitude is completely different" from Góngora's poems. In Rimbaud's poetry there is also a "criticism of reality and for the values that support it." Mallarmé, however, is something altogether different, as Paz indicates with enthusiasm. In fact, says Paz, Mallarmé is *the* key figure in the development of modern poetry.

Critics have long been fascinated by the stunning role that Mallarmé's work played as a precursor of the avant-garde movement. Seventy years later we can look at it as not only a forerunner of current philosophical and self-reflective verse, but also a likely nonexhaustible source of ever-new readings for future generations of writers. It is very useful to have Paz, here, begin to explain why it is possible to see so much in the French Symbolist's fairly small body of published work. First of all, Paz claims that Mallarmé is, in his terms, more "rigorous" than Rimbaud.[5] He then goes on to make this parenthetical comment on Mallarmé's *oeuvre:* "if that is the proper word for a few signs left on a handful of pages, the traces of an unparalleled joining of exploration and a shipwreck." This description could be seen as a definition of certain contemporary poets' own texts. Specifically, as we will be seeing in the following chapters, these poets will be "exploring" both the disintegration of language and the ultimate failure (the shipwreck) that such a fatalistic undertaking presupposes—but always aware of the "traces" (and here Paz prefigures a term that is one of the keys to Jacques Derrida's theory of language) left in the wake of the poetic exploration into words and their workings. Paz's next insightful comment on Mallarmé's verse almost forces us to see his Symbolist poetry as a foretaste of the way that poststructuralists will look at language: "The word is the obverse side of reality: not nothingness but the Idea, the pure sign that no longer points to anything and is neither being nor nonbeing." Paz's statement is remarkably similar to this clear statement of the foundation of poststructuralism made by Christopher Norris in his book on *Deconstruction: Theory and Practice:*

> If there is a single theme which draws together the otherwise disparate field of "structuralist" thought, it is the principle—first enounced by

Saussure—that language is a *differential* network of meaning. There is no self-evident or one-to-one link between "signifier" and "signified," the word as (spoken or written) vehicle and the concept it serves to evoke.[6]

Paz's explication easily leads us to the conclusion that Mallarmé was already well aware of the distinction that the poststructuralists would later establish as fundamental—that the sign "no longer points to anything." The "neither being nor nonbeing" of the pure sign here also roughly corresponds to what Norris is describing with the word "*differential*" (his italics, which help to imply both its importance and its problematic nature). This "pure" sign, for the poststructuralists, will always *differ* from any sayable meaning, and thus any expressible meaning will always be *deferred,* a dual concept that Jacques Derrida, as is well known, has conflated into his French neologism, "différance." By no means am I trying to say that Paz is giving a deconstructionist reading of Mallarmé here, but he is clearly pointing out elements of Mallarmé that correspond closely with the deconstructionists' criticism of language.

In this essay Paz gives no explanation as to how he arrived at this summary of what is at the core of Mallarmé's work—the concept of the word as "pure sign"—but I believe that we can explain why this statement is so credible and at the same time so prescient. Paz's cryptic-looking sentence can, I think, be taken as a brilliant encapsulation of Mallarmé's magnificent poem, "Un coup de dés . . ." Perhaps the best way to back up this assertion is to make some specific comments on that poem, along the way showing how it foreshadows the development of some self-reflective poetry in Latin America.

"Un coup de dés jamais n'abolira le hasard" (A throw of the dice will never abolish chance), the whole title, is a collection of statements ("themes" and "subordinate themes," as Gerald Bruns calls them) scattered over twenty pages in various typographical formations and typefaces. Graphically, it is obviously a forerunner of Apollinaire's *calligrammes* and the poems of such avant-gardists as the Chilean Vicente Huidobro. One of the purposes of this physical disposition of the words on the page, besides giving a graphic equivalent of the dice throw (the words often seem to be tumbling off the right-hand side of the page), is to force the reader into a simultaneous reading of the various statements. There simply is no stable context to the poem. Nevertheless, if a truly comprehensive reading of the poem were even possible, it might well show that an almost poststructuralist view of language underlies the whole text, as Robert Greer Cohn suggests in various of his incisive commentaries.

A perspective on language is certainly contained in the items within the poem that are given explicit emphasis by their large type size. These truly large words seemingly scattered through the poem do seem to have the most "meaning" in this text, but so, ironically, do the words in the smallest, almost minute print. The title words, "A throw of the dice will never abolish chance," spread out over most of the twenty pages, are in the largest type size, dominating the poem. My reading (and it is just that; I make no claim for breaking new ground) sees the "throw of the dice" as a metaphor for the writing process itself: casting the words onto the page in a (perhaps vain) effort to beat the odds and create a text with a lasting meaning. The other emphasized (and oversized) items in the text, beginning with these two lines from the first pair of pages, support and enrich this reading:

EVEN WHILE TOSSED IN ETERNAL CIRCUMSTANCES
FROM THE DEPTHS OF A SHIPWRECK[7]

The utter despair this image produces frames and determines the text that is yet to be played out, in the sense of futility evoked by the eternal burial and in the evident failure implied by the shipwreck:

IT WAS THE NUMBER / DID IT EXIST / DID IT BEGIN AND DID IT END /
DID IT ADD UP / DID IT ILLUMINATE / THIS WOULD BE CHANCE

The number here—literally, seen as the uppermost side of the die—is a clear reference to the pure sign. It is the equivalent of, or a metaphor for, the word that turns up on the page (much the same role that the word "cifra" plays as the title of Jorge Luis Borges's last book of poetry). The questions that follow completely probe all aspects of this sign, after asking whether it even exists. The second and third questions—on whether it begins or ends— seem to prefigure one of the central concerns in Jacques Derrida's *De la grammatologie:* what he calls "a question of origin" of the linguistic sign.[8] The last two questions have to do with whether this sign has any effect or possible purpose. Fittingly, positioned beneath this series of questions is CHANCE; any result would implicitly be only fortuitous, a stroke of luck. If this seems pessimistic, the large-print words on the next two pages at first appear to be even more so:

NOTHING / WILL HAVE TAKEN PLACE / EXCEPT THE PLACE

However, given the poststructuralist view of language that we have already seen prefigured in "Un coup de des . . . ," these verses by Mallarmé can be seen as paralleling and foreseeing a deconstructionist approach to the text itself. This verse, in fact, is as good an illustration as we could find of Paul de Man's assertion that "poetic writing is the most advanced and refined mode of deconstruction; it may differ from critical or discursive writing in the economy of its articulation, but not in kind." Indeed, these briefest of lines also implicitly contain the central tenet of deconstruction as succinctly stated by de Man:

> The deconstruction is not something we have added to the text but it constituted the text in the first place. A literary text simultaneously asserts and denies the authority of its own rhetorical mode.[9]

The denial in the poem is clear: "nothing will have taken place." But so is the assertion that coexists with it. The word "except" totally undermines the concept of "nothing," and the repetition of the word "place," along with giving that word the final position (place), provides even more evidence that the activity has had importance. Even if a reader's first response to the above lines is to see only the negative result, on the next (and last) two pages we have these qualifying words:

EXCEPT PERHAPS A CONSTELLATION

The word "perhaps" perpetuates the sense of doubt that has colored this whole text, but the dice throw, or the author's placing words on the blank paper, may now have a result after all—a possibly rich one. For Robert Greer Cohn this verse shows that "we cannot ever reach absolute meaning but neither can we deny it is way out there somewhere."[10] A "constellation" can thus also be seen as a set of dots shining through that metaphysical darkness. It is, further, a group of sparkling stars that form (or suggest) an image in the sky. Or (in French at least) a cluster of bright stones set in a piece of jewelry. Thinking back to the image on the first pages of the poem, the stars that form this constellation could be seen as a way to cope with the "eternal circumstances" that looked only depressing in that first context. And these same stars, as guides for the mariner's compass, could be a reprieve from the shipwreck that was also part of that same image. Certainly the brightness of the stars in the constellation implies a positive answer to the earlier question: "Did it illuminate?" Even more important than the relatively positive final image with which "Un coup de des . . ." ends is the *type* of poetry it prefigures. Indeed, "Mallarmé offers his poem as the model of a new genre," says Paz in another key essay from 1965, "Signs in Rotation." What it models is what Paz, following Mallarmé, calls the "critical poem." This term, we will see, incorporates the textual principles that also coincide with the fundamental ideas of deconstruction theory that we have been alluding to and that I take as the central tenet of my book. As Paz himself explains:

> A critical poem: if I am not mistaken, the union of these two contradic-
> tory words means: that poem that contains its own negation and that
> makes of that negation the point of departure for the song, equally
> distant from affirmation and negation. Poetry . . . denies itself each
> time it is realized in a poem—unless the poem is simultaneously a
> criticism of that attempt. The negation of the negation annuls the absur-
> dity and dissolves chance.[11]

For a poem to "contain its own negation" and "to deny itself" implies that the author has been *aware* of the problems inherent in creating a poetic text. The principal source of difficulty for Mallarmé and for the "critical" writers who follow his lead is language. As we have seen, the poststructuralist theorists also point out that language—the concept of the sign—no longer allows for transmitting a fixed meaning. By drawing attention to their awareness of a fallible language, and of the irony inherent in continuing to use that language, the critical poets are able to go beyond the impasse that would otherwise overwhelm them. The act of negation, of pointing out the problems and even the impossibilities confronting them, becomes the source of this new and exploratory verse, the new "song" (an ironic term in itself, implying as it does a free, lyrical, and carefree melody).

Paz emphasizes that Mallarmé's poetry—and the more contemporary work it prefigures—*is* difficult, a difficulty he classifies as a "moral" one, since it "implies a negation of the outer world . . . as in philosophical reflection." Here again Paz is making my job easier, by expressing in such simple terms a basic premise of this study: that many of the poets to be studied here are to an extent working on problems usually considered central to the philosophy of language. What makes the exploration all the more impressive is that these philosophical concerns are all subsumed into their "critical poetry," with no detriment to their aesthetic value as poetic texts. As we will see in the next chapter, Paz's own poetry is a textbook example of the critical poetry that he explains so clearly and convincingly.

Paz does not suggest *why* poets would even take up this kind of self-conscious poetry, admitting that those who dismiss the quest as "utter madness are legion." Yet he gives supreme praise to those who have ventured into this territory: "Nonetheless, for more than a century a few solitary spirits, among them the noblest and most gifted human beings who have ever trod this earth, have unhesitatingly devoted their entire lives to this absurd undertaking." That final sentence in Paz's essay gives no indication of whom he might include among the "solitary spirits." One can point, however, to some important poets from both Spain and Latin America who have preceded the current vein of "thinking" poets.

Although no poet from Spain foresaw the current preoccupation with the failure of language in the concentrated way that Mallarmé did, there are a few glimmers of this kind of critical concern, leading up to the present. Currently there is at least one Spanish poet whose concerns parallel those of the recent Latin American writers who form the basis of this study; that is Jaime Siles (born in 1951). In texts from *Música de agua* (Water music) (1981) and *Columnae* (1985), Siles demonstrates a lack of confidence in language almost matching the level of despair that characterizes the work of Roberto Juarroz, the most skeptical of the Latin American critical poets. For example, we have these lines that begin "Textualidad en comas" (Textuality between commas):

> El lenguaje es columna
> interior de la nada.
> Es un hueco en el aire,
> una gota en el agua
>
> o vacío vertido
> en dados de palabras,
> en sintagmas, en signos,
> en fonemas, en largas
>
> sucesiones de letras
> sin idioma, borradas.[12]
>
> [Language is an interior
> column of nothing.
> It is a hollow in the air,
> a drop on the water

or an emptiness poured out
into the words' dice,
into sintagmas, into signs,
into phonemes, into long

successions of letters
without language, erased.]

Pessimistic in the extreme, these lines repeatedly describe language and its words as being nothing ("nothing," "hollow," "emptiness"), and finally abolished ("erased"). Prior to Siles, there have been only scattered examples of true uneasiness with regard to language. José Angel Valente and other members of his generation of 1956–71,[13] such as Claudio Rodríguez and Gloria Fuertes, refer often to language in their poems, but their concerns are about the limitations or types of poetic language, and they do not really find themselves in a crisis. If we go back almost to Mallarmé's time, we can find a reflection of his concerns about language in an early poem by Juan Ramón Jiménez. Jiménez began as a Symbolist at the turn of the century, and his later texts, like Valéry's, revolve around his famous search for a "pure poetry."

True, the verses we most associate with this "poesía desnuda" seem to imply a perfect poetic language, the "sufficient" language that Mayhew discusses, as in these famous first lines from poem number 3 of *Eternidades:*

¡Intelijencia, dame
el nombre exacto de las cosas![14]

[Intelligence, give me
the exact name of things]

But there is one full poem of Jiménez's that I would like to examine briefly. It is a compelling reflection of Mallarmé's "Un coup de dés . . ." Poem number 11 from *Laberinto* (1911) is in notable ways still a Symbolist text, as is Mallarmé's, with its many musical references, examples of synesthesia, and suggestions of a hidden idea. Note, however, the quadruple metaphor in the first four lines, linking the poet's working with words ("la frente") to the words displayed on the paper, then to the words seen as stars reflecting in the sky, and finally to a "labyrinth of bells":

Como en un río quieto, en el papel la frente
refleja, quieta, las palabras

que vibran en sus cielos, cual las notas de estrellas
de un laberinto de campanas.
Notas que van formando, luz a luz, son a son,
rosa a rosa, lágrima a lágrima,
no sé qué arquitectura encendida y cantante,
ablandada de luna de alma.
Fin sin fin de una rota armonía sin nombre,
jamás, en la idea apagada;
hojas secas, cristales de color, flores únicas
que, entre las sombras, se entrelazan.
Un ¿qué? del más allá, que llega hasta la vida
por veredas trasfiguradas,
cual una aurora errante, que en los cielos del sueño
dejase atrás polen de plata.[15]

[As in a calm river, the forehead calmly
reflects, on the paper, the words
that vibrate in their heavens, like the notes of stars
from a labyrinth of bells.
Notes that are forming, light by light, sound by sound,
rose by rose, tear by tear,
I don't know what kind of bright and singing architecture,
softened by the moon of the soul.
End without end of a nameless broken harmony,
never closed off in the idea;
dry leaves, crystals in color, unique flowers
that, in the shadows, intertwine.
A "what?" from beyond, that even reaches life
by transfigured paths,
like an errant dawn, that in the heavens of sleep
leaves behind silver pollen.]

That extended metaphor at the beginning of the text firmly establishes its metapoetic nature. Although the rest of the lines seemingly refer only to resonances from either stars or bells, the larger
reference is clearly to the written text. In line 5 we see that the
"notes" forming this symphonic text are composed of ephemeral
elements: light, sounds, roses, tears. And they come together into
an equally indefinite text: "un no sé qué arquitectura." Line 9—
with its "end without end," "broken harmony," and "name-
lessness"—gives a multiple impression of the complete displacement of any unity or fixed impression from this process. Indeed,
the result, in line 13, is a "what?"—the result of "transfigured"
paths and "errant" auroras, terms that reinforce the indefiniteness
of both the naming and signifying processes. The "silver pollen"

at the end of the text could well be seen as an image of what
Mallarmé's "constellation" might "leave behind."

This metaphorical text sees the poem as an ephemeral construction, built out of the most fragile and imprecise elements. But
rather than the anguish that pervades most of "Un coup de des
. . . ," this brief text emphasizes the uncertain but shimmering
words ("que vibran") and the luminous images and ideas that they
can generate. This kind of positive perspective colors most of the
texts by Juan Ramón Jiménez that ruminate on language. Although
several of his poems question language, his poetry is not yet "critical" in Paz's terms, as it shows a tendency toward a desire for a
"sufficient" poetic language.

Another Spanish poet who is known to have a certain concern
for language is Gerardo Diego, often linked to the *creacionista*
movement begun by the Chilean Vicente Huidobro, himself, as we
will see, a precursor of the critical trend. Diego's texts, like those
of other Spanish poets, most often express a concern for a sufficient poetic language. There is one early poem—from 1918, when
he was twenty-two years old—that also echoes Mallarmé. The
poem has a title, "Poeta sin palabras" (Poet without words), that
looks like a perfect synthesis of the critical poets' dilemma. The
first strophe (of six) also looks as if it could be foreseeing the
anguish many of the later "thinking" poets evoke.

> Voy a romper la pluma. Ya no la necesito.
> Lo que mi alma siente yo no lo sé decir.
> Persigo la palabra y sólo encuentro un grito
> roto, inarticulado, que nadie quiere oír.[16]

> [I'm going to break my pen. I don't need it any more.
> What my soul feels I don't know how to say.
> I pursue the word and only find a broken
> inarticulate cry that no one wants to hear.]

The word seen as a broken cry certainly seems to be foreshadow-
ing the most pessimistic verses of Roberto Juarroz or David
Huerta, or at least Vicente Huidobro's epic *Altazor,* with its totally
incoherent ending. But in the following verses Diego's poem calls
for a poet to grant the speaker an ability to "truly say beautiful
things." Then in the final strophe comes this prayer for the gift of
poetic speech:

> Tú, Señor, que a los mudos ordenabas hablar,
> y ellos te obedecían. Pues mi alma concibe

bellas frases sin forma, házmelas tú expresar.
Ordénale ya "Habla" al poeta que en mí vive.

[You, Lord, who ordered the mute to speak,
and they obeyed you. Since my soul conceives
of beautiful phrases without form, make me express them.
Give the order to "Speak" to the poet who lives in me.]

It is taken for granted, in these last lines, that there is a perfectly
acceptable, adequate poetic language available to the writer, and
that it just needs to be found. Divine inspiration would help, but
only to find the shapely phrases that the poet thinks he needs. The
only thing worrying the poet is how to write the best possible
poetry. There is no doubt that the resulting words will be effective.

If there is thus no real follower of Mallarmé's questioning bent
in Spain, at least until the most recent generation, are there any
such precursors of critical poetry in the first part of the twentieth
century in Latin America? First of all we must say that there was
a huge amount of French influence on Latin American poetry in
the late nineteenth century, but it was not from the philosophical
and apparently hermetic branch of Symbolism that Mallarmé represented. Rather, Rubén Darío and the other *modernistas* looked
toward the art-for-art's-sake approach modeled by Verlaine and
the other more aesthetically involved nineteenth-century French
poets, such as LeConte de Lisle, Catulle Mendès, and later Jules
Laforgue. With the avant-garde movements, and their influences,
that came to Latin America in the 1920s, however—chiefly Ultraism, Creationism, and Surrealism—came the attitude of testing
poetry's limits. As "far out" as their experimentation into metaphor and image often was ("más allá" was the rallying cry for the
Ultraists), it was based on a language seen as a stable medium.
Two poets from this period start to be concerned about poetry's
underpinnings and have had a huge impact on their successors.
When I asked most of the poets included in this book who their
influences had been, almost all of them mentioned the same two
Latin American poets as having most inspired them as they began
their careers: César Vallejo (Perú, 1892–1938) and Vicente Huidobro (Chile, 1893–1948). Guillermo Sucre, a master critic of Latin
American poetry—in a brief essay titled "Una poesía escéptica de
sí misma" (A poetry skeptical of itself)—also singles out these
same two poets as being the first to consciously take on what he
calls "the problem of language."[17] Interestingly enough, Vallejo,
apart from a few well-known poems that would indicate both a
fascination and a frustration with language, deals little in overt

metapoetry. There are some poems in *Trilce* (1922) where the poet is playing with language, possibly in synch with the avant-garde movements then in full bloom in Europe, or even possibly in "an attempt to find a 'deconstructionist' language," in the view of Jean Franco. A lingering distrust of language also colors much of his poetry, according to Franco,[18] which Sucre also notes, commenting that Vallejo was afraid that his language would be reduced either to "pure convention" or to mere commentary. But probably the main reason Vallejo is thought of in terms of language are some famous first lines to a few of his poems, most notably this self-explanatory pair:

> ¡Y si después de tantas palabras,
> no sobrevive la palabra![19]

> [And if after so many words,
> the word does not survive!]

Also, the poem "Intensidad y altura" (Intensity and height) (from 1937) begins with this line: "Quiero escribir, pero me sale espuma" (I want to write, but out comes foam),[20] and continues on, through plays on words, to show the indecisiveness of writing. In addition to these poems about poetry that have stimulated the critical poets, there had to be something about Vallejo to make him such a powerful influence on almost all the poets to be studied here. That something is certainly the strong moral component of his verse, most notably seen in its social criticisms and its corresponding search for justice. This will be seen as ironic by those who tend to criticize "intellectual" literature as irrelevant at best, especially in those Latin American countries which have such persistent social, economic, and political problems. Roberto Juarroz, the most philosophical and critical of all the poets in this study, sums up all too succinctly the root of those problems: "Hemos llegado a una situación trágica: la sociedad, que debía proteger al hombre, le ha mentido y lo ha traicionado" (We have gotten into a tragic situation: society, which ought to protect people, has lied to and betrayed them). Poetry, precisely because it is a deep human response, is thus of indispensable social value. For this reason, as Juarroz often points out, a true commitment by a writer to his or her poetry is an "ethical" one. Poetry goes to the deepest core of human consciousness, where it counteracts the chaos and corruption that afflict society, as Juarroz explains:

El poeta no habla a la sociedad sino al hombre, de soledad a soledad, de silencio a silencio, de ser a ser. La sociedad es ruido, campo de concentración más o menos disimulado, exaltación del lucro y el poder, malversación del hombre. La poesía es, en cambio, el mayor respeto al hombre.[21]

[The poet does not speak to society but to people, from solitude to solitude, from silence to silence, from being to being. Society is noise, a more or less disguised concentration camp, an exaltation of money and power, a bad investment of people. Poetry, on the other hand, is the greatest respect for people.]

The other "thinking" poets share this concern for grappling with the deepest *human* issues, which transcend the immediate problems of society. It is true that most of these more philosophical poets generally do not write particularly socially conscious or rabble-rousing poems. There are exceptions, however. Alfredo Veiravé, along with some good "critical poetry," has written poems critical of the government at both the regional and the national levels in Argentina; some of these have drawn exceptional response. And Gonzalo Millán, from Chile, who is one of the most important intellectual poets, is best known as a socially directed one. It is safe to say that the spirit of Vallejo, especially his moral essence, lives on in these "thinking" poets, as Juarroz calls them.

A more evident influence on these poets came from Vicente Huidobro, the Chilean founder of the avant-garde movement "Creacionismo." There is no doubt that Huidobro was completely taken with the topic of language. His many manifestos speak often of the poet's duty to use a special language in order to "create." Most of these pronouncements, and applications of them in his poetic texts, clearly fall into the category of "arbitrary" or "poetic" language, as described by Mayhew. That is, Huidobro, beginning with his famous "Arte poética" (from 1918), preaches the ability of poetic language to create "new worlds." "The poet is a little god" is one of his best-known lines, and in "Poeta," the speaker announces that he plays "the official flute."[22]

But for all the confidence, even bravado, that Huidobro shows with regard to poetic language (and many of these "creacionista" poems do work as they were intended), there are some indications of doubt. An example, from *Ver y palpar* (Seeing and feeling) (1941), is the aptly titled "Preceptiva funesta" (Fatal precept) an expression of despair over language, especially as captured in these two lines:

> Las palabras se cargan y se descargan día y noche
> Soy la angustia eres la angustia[23]

> [Words load up and unload day and night
> I am anguish you are anguish]

The words' endless "loading and unloading" points to a certain aimlessness, particularly since it is followed by the double expression of anguish.

For a literary scream of anguish over the failure of even poetic language, however, we only have to go to Huidobro's well-known experimental epic poem, *Altazor*. According to René de Costa, indefatigable student of the Huidobro "archive," this long poem became for Huidobro a way to resolve the "aesthetic problem" he perceived behind the reliance on metaphors that characterized Cubist poetry and that resulted in "imagistic layering" in anything other than a short poem. Although the poem's central concern can be seen as metaphysical, "the urge to arrive at the meaning of life, metaphorized here as a fall into oblivion,"[24] the "aesthetic" problem of poetic language is clearly at the forefront, especially in the later cantos.

In *Altazor* the speaker is in outer space, engaged in a free fall toward earth. The metapoetic focus of the poem begins in the preface, when "Altazor," the poem's mythical "protagonist," his parachute having gotten tangled on a star, jots down a few "profound thoughts," including this one: "un poema es una cosa que nunca ha sido, que nunca podrá ser" (a poem is a thing that never has been, that never will be able to be),[25] prefiguring a nihilistic denouement for this particular poem as linguistic experiment. Beginning with Canto 3, then, the poem becomes, borrowing freely from de Costa's authoritative and succinct analysis, "a trek through the blind alleys of linguistic experimentation," following a constant procedure: "a particular linguistic possibility is used and abused, pushed to its limits," thus going "from being a text that discourses on the limits of poetry to one that actually demonstrates those limits." In the final Canto, *Altazor* presents what de Costa appropriately calls a system of "de-writing," a process of creating a language characterized by progressive non-sense, ending in two pages of apparent gibberish of this type:

> Ai aia aia
> ia ia ia aia ui

For de Costa this finale is a "primal scream," and I would agree up to a point, adding that at the same time it could be an expression of the poet's frustration with what he sees as a completely failed language. This reversion to "language" as pure sound, unrelated to any semantic point of reference, is also, much like a primal scream, a return to a type of pre-sense, to a pure "gut-level" expression unencumbered with any attempt at meaning.

Since Huidobro had formed himself as a Cubist-Creationist, mainly in Europe, and was familiar with all of the different movements' attempts to outdo and go beyond the others with respect to artistic limits, this poem can be seen in part as a continuation of avant-garde experimentation, carried out to an aesthetic impasse. But it is also clearly a vision of a failed language, which sets the stage for the critical poets.

Failed language is indeed, to one degree or another, shared by all of the poets to be examined in the coming chapters, although they certainly do not allow themselves the luxury of the out-of-control free fall that Huidobro's text portrays. Rather, these more recent writers think through the crisis of language they confront. They attempt, in spite of the contradictions this implies, to provide a comprehensive (or at least comprehensible) picture of this dilemma.

2
Octavio Paz and the Magic of the Word

LONG considered one of the preeminent poets in Latin America, Octavio Paz (Mexico, 1914) is known for his innovative and probing verse. As mentioned before, Paz was the first Latin American poet to focus on the question of language—a concern that various other writers have made the center of their own works over the last three decades. But if Paz is an important innovator in this area, he also serves as a bridge between earlier tendencies and the most recent movement. As we have seen, he recalled a Symbolist poet who was ahead of *his* time, citing Mallarmé's work as the touchstone for a poetry that questions its own construction. But he also adopted another source of influence that should, one might think, have little relationship to the philosophical problems of language. This second source was Surrealism, and in particular its originator André Breton, who significantly, according to Paz, was a passionate reader of Mallarmé.[1]

Both of the Latin American poets discussed in the last chapter as possible precursors of a concern for language were notably associated with the vanguard. César Vallejo showed, along with a certain preoccupation with language, a marked interest in inventive metaphors and images, in line with the prevailing avant-garde aesthetic. Vicente Huidobro, who was associated with Pierre Reverdy and French Cubism and was the creator of the movement called Creationism, embodied the avant-garde spirit even as a very young man. Rather than looking to these earlier manifestations of the avant-garde in Latin America, however, Octavio Paz instead turned to what was to be its final evolution, Breton's Surrealism. In this, Paz is not alone. Actually, Breton and his movement have had several waves of followers in different Latin American countries. The most important of these were three "cycles" of Surrealism in Argentina (beginning with Aldo Pellegrini in the 1920s and in later manifestations led most notably by Enrique Molina) and the "Mandrágora" group in Chile, led by Braulio Arenas.

Critics disagree, however, about the degree to which Paz himself could actually be labeled a Surrealist. The most concentrated look at Octavio Paz's connections with Surrealism is probably to be found in Jason Wilson's book, *Octavio Paz: A Study of His Poetics*. Wilson convincingly shows that Paz's "actitud vital" has strong affinities with the Surrealist program. But even though Wilson catalogs a few instances of the Mexican poet's participation in relatively "official" Surrealist events, such as as his publishing in a Surrealist anthology and his signing a 1951 manifesto, Wilson views Paz's specific links to Breton's movement as a general attitude ("poetry as wisdom"), along with some scattered stylistic similarities.[2] In a much briefer essay, Alejandra Pizarnik, an Argentine poet in her own right whose work we will study in a later chapter and who had substantial Surrealist grounding, said it best: "I would not say—in spite of how often it has been proclaimed— that Octavio Paz is a Surrealist. But I repeat: he is an unclassifiable poet in spite of being rooted in the most beautiful conquests of surrealism: the marvelous, the oneiric world, the passionate search for freedom."[3] Saúl Yurkiévich adds the explicit and useful observation that "Paz accepts the assumptions of Surrealism, [which] imply the belief in the magical powers of the word, in a suprareality."[4] Implicit in Surrealist poetics, as it was in the theories of all the other avant-garde movements, is a desire to stretch the limits of poetry and art, and Paz's affinities with the movement include that fascination with limits.

In the case of Surrealism, the limits on art (and life) were to be transcended, literally, by the creation of a sur-reality—a state beyond reality. In fact, in Paz's words, Breton "made no distinction between magic and poetry" (*AC,* 50). In important ways, Paz's poetry also points to such a new, magical reality. But this does not simply happen with a figurative wave of the wand. From his earliest poems, well before he appropriates Mallarmé's concept of the critical poem, one of Paz's concerns has been the problem of language—an inability to control words and their function. Two poems from the early 1940s show both this preoccupation with language and the Surrealist influence we have been talking about. The first indicates in its very title a concern with language and meaning.

PALABRA

Palabra, voz exacta
y sin embargo equívoca;
oscura y luminosa;

herida y fuente: espejo;
espejo y resplandor;
resplandor y puñal,
vivo puñal amado,
ya no puñal, sí mano suave: fruto.

Llama que me provoca;
cruel pupila quieta
en la cima del vértigo;
invisible luz fría
cavando en mis abismos,
llenándome de nada, de palabras,
cristales fugitivos
que a su prisa someten mi destino.

Palabra ya sin mí, pero de mí,
como el hueso postrero,
anónimo y esbelto, de mi cuerpo;
sabrosa sal, diamante congelado
de mi lágrima oscura.

Palabra, una palabra, abandonada,
riente y pura, libre,
como la nube, el agua,
como el aire y la luz,
como el ojo vagando por la tierra,
como yo, si me olvido.

Palabra, una palabra,
la última y primera,
la que callamos siempre,
la que siempre decimos,
sacramento y ceniza.

Palabra, tu palabra, la indecible,
hermosura furiosa,
espada azul, eléctrica,
que me toca en el pecho y me aniquila.[5]

[WORD

Word, exact voice
but still ambiguous;
dark and luminous
wound and source: mirror;
mirror and brightness

brightness and blade,
a live and loved blade,
no longer a blade but a smooth hand: fruit.

Flame that provokes me;
cruel quiet pupil
at the height of vertigo;
invisible cold light
digging into my abysses,
filling me with nothing, with words,
fugitive crystals
that in their haste subdue my fate.

Word not without me, but of me,
like the last bone
in my body, slim and anonymous;
flavorful salt, frozen diamond
of my dark tear.

Word, a word, abandoned,
smiling and pure, free,
like the cloud, like water,
like air and light,
like the eye wandering over the earth,
like me, if I forget.

Word, a word,
the first and the last,
the one we always keep silent,
the one we always say,
sacrament and ashes.

Word, your word, the unsayable,
furious beauty,
blue, electric sword,
that touches me on the chest and destroys me.]

The first two lines do two things: they establish a contradictory attitude toward the word, or the concept of the word, and they begin a series of explicit contradictions, or antinomies. The use of antinomies, of course, is a frequent device in André Breton's writings. Most of them here are apostrophes or metaphors for the title, "Word": *herida/fuente, resplandor/puñal, llama/pupila, cavando/llenando, sin mí/de mí, última/primera, callamos/decimos, sacramento/ceniza* (wound/source, brightness/blade, flame/pupil, digging/filling, without me/of me, final/first, we keep silent/we say, sacrament/ashes). This series of images made out of opposing terms serves as a good example of how Paz's metaphors function as what Lelia Madrid calls "minimal dialectic units." For Madrid, the central element in Paz's writing is the metaphor, precisely because it forms "a contradiction that is constantly being reborn."[6] She explains that while the two terms of any metaphor do coexist, the distance between them is never closed, causing a never-ending contradiction. In this poem, the many pairs of contradictory terms also serve as surprisingly complex and interrelating images or metaphors of the word.

To explain how these images work, we can look at the first two sets of antinomies: *herida/fuente, resplandor/puñal* (wound/fountain, brightness/blade). A wound damages, cuts open, but it also is the origin of color, heat, and movement in the blood that escapes from it, as well as a possible cause of death; a fountain or spring is a source of cool, clear, life-giving water. The brightness/blade pairing also has a life-versus-death tension inherent in it— the dagger being an obvious cause of injury or death, recalling the wound image, while the brightness could either be a metonym for the blade itself (the gleam that glances off it) or a single ray of light, in the form of a blade, that illuminates a situation. In the text these, and the rest of the images that spring from the other antinomies, all serve as pictures of how a word can function. But all of these seemingly contradictory images also undermine any notion of predictability with regard to a word. A word's meaning is presented as ranging from one extreme to another, so that any idea of a fixed reference seems to be eliminated. And—ironically, in this poem about words not being able to say anything concrete— there is a clear indicator in the text that points to the words' lack of substance: "filling me with nothing, with words." At the same time, of course, in this constant play of opposites, we also have the word referred to as "smiling and pure, free." But that freedom, in the next lines, only reinforces the intangibility and the indeterminacy of a word—as it is equated with the fluid, constantly moving cloud, water, air, and light, followed by the "wandering" gaze. The last stanza makes for an ingenious possible twist to an otherwise rather intellectual and sophisticated poem—as "your" word could refer to a woman's; here the poet now transforms all the earlier references to fascination and indeterminacy into a young woman's deigning to speak to him, an act that, in the last line, "blows him away." The "tu," however, could also refer to the poetic voice, or to his muse, and this second reading simply concludes the poet's fatal attraction to the ever-elusive poetic word.

What is interesting in this early poem is, for purposes of this study, Paz's fascination with the word, the basic element of language. But what also makes this poem so fascinating is its brilliant intermixing of the Surrealist use of antinomies and image with a playful Baroque tone, overlaid with a Romantic intensity. The next poem, from the same early period, is more self-consciously literary, in its complex interplay of images and in its references to Mallarmé.

ARCOS

A Silvina Ocampo

¿Quién canta en las orillas del papel?
Inclinado, de pechos sobre el río
de imágenes, me veo, lento y solo,
de mí mismo alejarme: oh letras puras,
constelacion de signos, incisiones
en la carne del tiempo, ¡oh, escritura,
raya en el agua!

        Voy entre verdores
enlazados, voy entre transparencias,
entre islas avanzo por el río,
por el río feliz que se desliza
y no transcurre, liso pensamiento.
Me alejo de mí mismo, me detengo
sin detenerme en una orilla y sigo,
río abajo, entre arcos de enlazadas
imágenes, el río pensativo.

Sigo, me espero allá, voy a mi encuentro,
río feliz que enlaza y desenlaza
un momento de sol entre dos álamos,
en la pulida piedra se demora,
y se desprende de sí mismo y sigue,
río abajo, al encuentro de sí mismo.

                        (*Libertad*, 35–36)

[ARCHES

Who sings on the edges of the paper?
Leaning over, facing the river
of images, I see myself, slowly and alone,
step away from myself: ah, pure letters,

constellation of signs, incisions
in the flesh of time, ah, writing,
a line in the water!

                              I move among the braided
greenery, I move among transparencies,
among the islands, I move along the river
on the happy river that slides along
and doesn't pass by, a smooth thought.
I step away from myself, I stop
without stopping on a bank and continue,
down the river, among the arches of braided
images, down the thoughtful river.

I keep on, I wait for myself there, I go to meet myself,
happy river that braids and unbraids
a moment of sun between two poplars,
it pauses on the smooth stone,
and separates from itself and goes on,
down the river, in search of itself.]

What we have here is an image of a man leaning over a river, and the reflection of that image in a river. Since in this poem the river is a metaphor for the text, the man reflected is the author, and the river or text reflects his relation to, and separation from, the poem, as well as reflecting the river's own composition. In poetic terms, the first line is a Mallarméan question, asking what effect the blank spaces around the words could have on the poem, as well as where the poetic voice comes from. This question is answered in the next lines with an image developed out of other images. To the question of "who sings?" the poetic voice answers "I see myself." The text, the "river of images," reflects its own author, but the author sees himself going away—an obvious reference to his losing control over the meaning of a text he has just written. What floats away, in this river of mental pictures, are the "pure letters," referring to an idealized language of pure signifiers making up the "constellation of signs," an image that comes straight from Mallarmé's landmark poem. After this pointed reference to "Un coup de dés . . ." it is not surprising to see the first stanza end with the despairing vision of writing seen as a momentary line drawn in the water.

Far from despair, however, the next stanza projects a hypnotic pastoral scene out of this river of images. The speaker goes along the now happy river, which slides along—continuing the metaphor of the text as river—with the author as reader slipping from image (island) to image. This process is repeated as he continues down the "thoughtful river" among the braided images arching over him (a verbal picture echoed years later in these lines from *Pasado en claro* (The past seen clearly): "el dios sin nombre . . . pasa entre los ramajes que escribo" (the god without name . . . goes among the branches that I write).[7] But as he slips farther away from himself he "stops without stopping," thus indicating the impossibility of seizing a fixed reference in this voyage through the text.

The final stanza reinforces the representation of the text as continual process and undoing: braiding and unbraiding something brilliant but intangible, "a moment of sun." That this continual doing and undoing is a never-ending process is made clear in the final image, as the river stops, then pulls away from itself—the text undoing itself once again—but then continues on in a "search for itself": a search for new readings of its "constellation of signs." The word undoing itself is also the topic of several poems in *Salamandra* (Salamander) (1962), a major book published almost two decades after those early poems. *Salamandra*, in fact, for Carmen Ruiz Barrionuevo, is the book that best represents Paz's attitude of "ruptura con la palabra" (breaking off with the word). The two most important poems that deal specifically with language here have indicative titles: "The Written Word" and "The Spoken Word." The first begins with these lines that clearly point out language's contradictory nature:

> Ya escrita la primera
> Palabra (nunca la pensada
> Sino la otra—ésta
> Que no la dice, que la contradice,
> Que sin decirla esta diciéndola)[8]

> [Now written the first
> Word (never the one you thought of
> But rather the other one—this one
> That doesn't say it, that contradicts it,
> That without saying it is saying it)]

The second develops this view of the contradictions inherent in language into a particular impasse that illustrates a specific way in which words really do work against each other.

LA PALABRA DICHA

> La palabra se levanta
> De la página escrita.

La palabra,
Labrada estalactita,
Grabada columna
Una a una letra a letra.
El eco se congela
En la página pétrea.
     Anima,
Blanca como la página,
Se levanta la palabra.
Anda
Sobre un hilo tendido
Del silencio al grito,
Sobre el filo
Del decir estricto.
El oído: nido
O laberinto del sonido.
Lo que dice no dice
Lo que dice: ¿cómo se dice
Lo que no dice?
          Di
Tal vez es bestial la vestal.
    Un grito
En un cráter extinto:
En otra galaxia
¿Como se dice ataraxia?
Lo que se dice se dice
Al derecho y al revés.
Lamenta la mcnte
De menta demente:
Cementerio es sementerio,
Simiente no miente.
      Laberinto del oído,
Lo que dices se desdice
Del silencio al grito
Desoído.
     Inocencia y no ciencia:
Para hablar aprende a callar.

                 (*Salamandra*, 31–32)

[THE SPOKEN WORD

The word rises
From the written page.
The word,
Hand-formed stalactite
Engraved column
One by one letter by letter.

The echo freezes hard
To the rocky page.
                    Spirit,
White like the page,
The word rises up.
It walks
On a thread strung
Between silence and a scream,
On the thread
Of strict expression.
The ear: a nest
Or labyrinth of sound.
                    What speaks does not speak
What speaks: how does one say
What doesn't speak?
                              Say
Perhaps the vestal is bestial.
A scream
Is an extinct crater:
In another galaxy
How does one say ataraxia?
What one says is said
backward and forward.
The mind laments
By mint demented:
Cemetery is sementary,
Seed does not lie.
Labyrinth of the ear,
What you say is unsaid
Unheard
Between silence and scream.
                    Innocence and not science:
To speak learn to be silent.]

From the first lines it is obvious that, in spite of the title, the word
at issue here begins as a written one. Perhaps as a consequence of
that written, engraved beginning, the extended image of the words
in the poem is one of a solid, tangible presence that is also a dynamic and active one: the word rises and walks in the first two
sections. It is seen as a stalactite and as a column, whose echo
is also made tangible as a frozen element on the equally rock-
hard page.

In contrast to all that solidity, in the second section of verses
the word becomes spirit, but still visible, sharing the page's white-

ness. Then comes its tightrope act, illustrating its double balancing role: between silence and scream, as well as between different strict meanings.

The last twenty-one lines, mainly by the use of a series of homonyms—words with the same sounds but different meanings—show off language's contradictory character: "what it says it doesn't say." The next-to-last line, in the best of these puns, gives some consciously ingenuous advice for using words in the face of their duplicitous quality. The writer must be intentionally naive. But the last verse also points to a more difficult concept—that speech can only come from silence. Silence as a necessary component of language can be part of a fairly complex philosophical attitude toward words, as we will see in particular in the poetry of Alejandra Pizarnik. But we could also read this last line as a call for the writer to be more selective, to "speak" only when a word demands to be acknowledged.

It is precisely the need to use language that underlies Paz's next major poetic work, *Pasado en claro* (1978). In this great "poem of self-recognition," as José Miguel Oviedo describes it, the poet goes deeply into "his origins, his personal past, his intellectual formation, his relationship to Mexico, universal culture, and above all, himself."[9] As such, *Pasado en claro* is probably the work that is of most importance to Paz's poetics or, more correctly, his "archive," the term Enrico Mario Santí (after Foucault) would use. The poem calls up the poet's whole personal and artistic context—including, significantly, his experience with "Oriental" thought, reinforced by his stay in India from 1962–1968. That experience had an immediate effect on Paz's work; his 1969 poetry collection, *Ladera este* (Eastern slope), is suffused with Indian themes. Of more interest, with respect to the issues of critical poetry, are the essays he published in *Conjunciones y disyunciones* (Conjunctions and disjunctions) in 1969. These essays will help to clarify elements of Tantric Buddhism woven into parts of *Pasado en claro*. It is fascinating to see how the main concepts of Tantrism both strengthen and commingle with the Mallarméan and Surrealist elements of Paz's poetry up to this time, as Manuel Durán has pointed out rather specifically in his study of Oriental influences in *Ladera este*.[10] Besides interweaving all of these personal and conceptual elements, *Pasado en claro* ends up channeling the poetic voice's entire being into a relationship with language.

Very early in the poem we see images that present the poet's search rooted deeply in language, especially in these lines:

Relumbran las palabras en la sombra.
Y la negra marea de las sílabas
cubre el papel y entierra
sus raíces de tinta
en el subsuelo del lenguaje.[11]

[The words shine in the shadows.
and the black tide of syllables
covers the paper and buries
its inky roots
in the subsoil of language.]

It is into that dark "subsoil of language" that the poetic voice goes
looking for its own self. And language, even at the outset of the
poem, is already proving to be a murky "crystal ball" into which
he is looking for revelation:

Ni allá ni aquí: por esa linde
de duda, transitada
solo por espejeos y vislumbres,
donde el lenguaje se desdice,
voy al encuentro de mí mismo.

                                                        (11)

[Neither here nor there: along that border
of doubt, crossed
only by mirages and glimpses,
where language unsays itself,
I go in search of myself.]

Indefinite ("neither here nor there," "mirages," "glimpses") and
contradictory (unsaying itself), language projects only uncertainty,
as additional lines from the middle of this long poem underscore:

Los nombres acumulan sus imágenes.
Las imágenes acumulan sus gaseosas,
conjeturales confederaciones.
Nubes y nubes, fantasmal galope
de las nubes sobre las crestas
de mi memoria . . .

                                                        (25)

[Names accumulate their images.
Images accumulate their gaseous
conjectural confederations.

Clouds and clouds, phantasmal gallop
of the clouds on the crests
of my memory . . .]

The only images that names (or words) can conjure up here are, in every respect, cloudy. The term "cloud" is repeated three times, and they themselves are "conjectural configurations" and phantoms. But language is what the poet is working with and through, in spite of its opaqueness. The poet's involvement in his own words shows through both transparently and poetically in this brief sentence, also from the middle of the poem:

Mis palabras,
al hablar de la casa, se agrietan.

(27)

[My words
crack when they speak of the house.]

For all the philosophical implications of the poet's introspection through language, here we see a more traditional poetic figure, which underscores even more the deeply poetic process that the whole poem is describing. The poet says "my words crack," but what he is actually doing is transferring the sensitive emotional response that the house provokes in *him* to his words. This kind of nostalgic pathetic movement brings us to a more personal connection with the implied author.

If early in the poem the poet projects himself into his language, now the poetic voice is becoming completely subsumed by the words of the text. In the following lines from near the end of the poem the references to a new state of being at first quite obviously refer to the poet's search for fulfillment, but by the end of the eight verses the references clearly point to language. This transition, within these eight selected verses, also sums up how Paz's interest in "Oriental" thought has helped to clarify and focus elements already present in his earlier poetry.

Hay un estar tercero:
el ser sin ser, la plenitud vacía,
hora sin horas y otros nombres
con que se muestra y se dispersa
en las confluencias del lenguaje
no la presencia: su presentimiento.
Los nombres que la nombran dicen: *nada,*
palabra de dos filos, palabra entre dos huecos.

(40)

[There is a third state of being:
being without being, empty fullness,
time without hours and other names
with which one displays and disperses,
in the confluences of language,
not presence: its presentiment.
The names that name it say: *nothing,*
a word with two edges, a word between two empty spaces.]

First, it is important to see these lines as a synthesis of some of
the key elements of Tantric Buddhism that Paz discusses at some
length in *Conjunctions and Disjunctions*, because these concepts
lead into and strongly reinforce ideas that have been recurring
since his earliest poetry. "The prevailing idea is the confluence of
opposites,"[12] especially the underlying concept of emptiness and
fullness. The abolition or fusion of contraries, Paz writes, especially those of the phenomenal world and the transcendental world,
results in "an absolute in the form of a fullness of being for the
Hindu [Tantrist] and ineffable emptiness for the Buddhist." The
"being without being" in the above lines thus represents this absolute, perfect fullness *and* emptiness. This concept flows through
the next verses into the confluences of language—and the plays on
presence and absence that illustrate this apparently contradictory
"basic premise of Tantrism," as stated by Paz: "the abolition of
contraries—without suppressing them."[13] The word "nada" here
has two edges: it *is* absence and it *is* present, and it hovers or
slides amidst emptiness. This image also resonates perfectly with
the Mallarméan criticism of language, where the idea of semantic
correspondence between sign and referent is seen as an impossible
myth. These two voids on each side of the word "nada" could also
be the very ideas of absence and presence between which this and
other words teeter. A few lines later in the poem, conversations
are said to take place "between the bullseyes of discourse, in the
conjuration of images" (41). Again this could be a reference to
language of the *Tantras* characterized by a "mobility of . . . meanings, the continuous shifting of the signs and their meanings,"
where, in one example given by Paz, "the vulva is a lotus that is
emptiness that is wisdom" (65). That shifting "conjuration of images" (which also recalls the Surrealists' use of sexual imagery)
does not seem to allow for even an instantaneous pinpointing of
meaning. This picture of language functioning only *between* meanings also looks as if it were sliding within what Lacan would call
a "chain of signifieds."

In either case, the poetic voice here would apparently prefer to nail down a meaning for his words, as he says a few verses later:

> Quise nombrarlo
> con un nombre solar,
> una palabra sin revés.
>
> (42)

> [I wanted to name it
> with a solar name,
> a word without a reverse side.]

He finds, instead, as we see yet a few lines later, "pyramids of bones, verbal garbage heaps." Besides possibly invoking Tantric ritual ("eating the sacrament in its foul and impure form" while surrounded by bones, as Paz describes it), this image shows the words' lack of desired effect. Since words are obviously seen as dead and wasted, the poet does this:

> Alcé con las palabras y sus sombras
> una casa ambulante de reflejos,
> torre que anda, construcción de viento.
>
> (42–43)

> [I raised, with words and their shadows,
> an ambulating house of reflections,
> a tower that walks, a construction of wind.]

The image of a tower made of words shows just how ephemeral such a construction must be, and it is clearly a metaphor for any written text: its meaning cannot be pinned down—it is constantly in flux (the tower ambulates, walks) and built of intangible elements (shadows, reflections, wind). The shaky word-tower image is, then, this very text, as becomes clear a few lines later:

> Espiral de los ecos, el poema
> es aire que se esculpe y se disipa,
> fugaz alegoría de los nombres
> verdaderos. A veces la página respira:
> los enjambres de signos, las repúblicas
> errantes de sonidos y sentidos,
> en rotación magnética se enlazan y dispersan
> sobre el papel.
>
> (43)

[Spiral of echoes, the poem
is air that is sculpted and dissipates,
a fleeting allegory of real
names. At times the page breathes:
the swarm of signs, the errant
republics of sounds and meanings,
in a magnetic rotation they link together and disperse
on the page.]

For all the references to the ephemeral and intangible nature of
a word creation, the poem *is* a creation of some validity. First of
all, the use of the verb "ser" (to be) gives a sense of inherent
purpose, and that purpose is suggested by three words often associated with art. The poem is a spiral, a term often used by Paz to
suggest, beyond its visual beauty, a sense of continuous aspiration;
it is sculpted, which reinforces the sense of aesthetic form that was
given by the spiral, and further underscores the artistic creation
the poem is; and finally, it is an allegory—of real names—and here
the poet completes the picture. For the poem is, here, a verbal
image, sculpted out of words to hint at a meaning, however fleeting.
As a result of this fleeting verbal activity, the page breathes—it
lives, it functions. Curiously, the image used to describe the
poem's working is that of "magnetic rotation," which recalls the
Surrealist principle of *Les champs magnétiques* of Breton and Sou-
pault. It also brings to mind this definition of the poem, which Paz
gave in *The Bow and the Lyre:* "a magnetic object, a secret meeting
place of many opposing forces."[14] The words' magnetic force, their
ability to constantly interweave and disperse, as the text would
have it, allows them to create ever-changing meanings in ever-
changing contexts.

Finally, a few verses later, the poem ends with this much-cited
line: "Soy la sombra que arrojan mis palabras" (I am the shadow
that my words throw out). Behind this metaphor, and the image it
creates, is a clear return to Mallarmé and "Un coup de des. . ."
Throughout *Pasado en claro* the poetic voice has shown that it
depends on the written text for its existence, and in this final line
we see how the existence of the implied author, or the conception
of such a figure, is linked to the element of chance behind every
dice "throw" of his words.

Seen as a shadow, in this last line, the vision of the poetic figure
that the text had set out to draw ends up belying the two most
likely meanings of the poem's dense title, *Pasado en claro:* a clean
copy (of a text) or the past seen clearly. We see neither of those

as the text ends. As if following the basic premise of Tantrism, the abolition but not suppression of contraries, here the opposites light and dark are abolished, but not suppressed—they are commingled and flow together into the shadow. Thus, we and the poet are left with a *residue* (neither empty nor full), a shadowy trace of his past, which his words have left for us, by means of their spiral of fleeting images.

Shadows now start to make something clear. Even with all the difficulties that have been created by discarding the myth of the perfectly functioning sign, poems do work. We see this in the exquisite and elegant shadow that *Pasado en claro* does leave, as the text suggests in its last line. We see it even more specifically in several passages in Paz's poetry collection from two decades later, *Arbol adentro* (1987). Nothing could be clearer than these resigned but defiant lines:

> Las palabras son inciertas
> y dicen cosas inciertas.
> Pero digan esto o aquello,
> > > nos dicen.[15]

> [Words are uncertain
> and they say uncertain things.
> But whether they tell us this or that,
> > > they do tell us.]

Perhaps this is the poet's common sense showing through. After all, in 1956, in *The Bow and the Lyre,* Paz had said that "reserve toward language is an intellectual attitude," whereas "to trust language is man's spontaneous and original attitude" (40). In any case, this explains the irony of a writer complaining that words do not transmit the ideas that he wishes to send, yet continuing to use those words in writing. The words that he uses do have a function; they send signals, albeit uncertain ones.

A further positive spin on the recurrent concerns about language in Paz's earlier poetry comes in two poems dedicated to the famous linguistic theoretician, Roman Jakobson. Interestingly, in a speech that Paz gave at MIT in 1982 in memory of Jakobson's death that year, he observed, "The true theme of poetry, although always secret and never explicit, is poetry itself" (*Arbol adentro,* 179). This statement applies in particular, of course, to what Paz called the "critical poem." These poems dedicated to Jakobson are critical ones in every way. Explicitly about poetry, they express a persistent doubt as to its ability to say anything, yet they paradoxically admit that an opening for a new type of meaning is created. As such overtly critical texts, these poems also bring us back to Paz's comments on Mallarmé, and at the same time incorporate Bretonian antinomies that recall his fascination with both French Surrealism and Eastern religions. The first of this pair of texts revolves around an awareness of the poetic process and the crisis that that now presupposes.

DECIR:HACER

Entre lo que veo y digo,
entre lo que digo y callo,
entre lo que callo y sueño,
entre lo que sueño y olvido,
la poesía.
                    Se desliza
entre el sí y el no:
                                dice
lo que callo,
                    calla
lo que digo,
                    sueña
lo que olvido.
                    No es un decir:
es un hacer.
                    Es un hacer
que es un decir.
                    La poesía
se dice y se oye:
                                es real.
Y apenas digo
                    es real,
se disipa.
                    ¿Asi es más real?

                                                    (11–12)

[SAYING:DOING

Between what I see and I say,
between what I say and I don't say,
between what I dream and I forget,
poetry.
                    It slides
between yes and no:
                                it says

what I don't say,
               it keeps silent
what I say,
          it dreams
what I forget.
               It isn't saying:
it's doing.
                    It's doing
that is saying.
                    Poetry
is said and is heard:
                    it is real.
And I barely say
                    it is real,
and it slips away.
                    Is it more real this way?]

"Between," the first word of each of the opening lines, indicates at least a partial resolution to the crisis that the various contradictory elements of the poem would otherwise imply. It is not a question of either/or with respect to seeing or saying, saying or not saying, yes or no. Poetry "slides between" these oppositions, as the text says, and as it slides between, it both says *and* does. The poetic text is thus defined as an active process that, specifically in the final verses here, questions its own validity. There is no doubt, though, that the question in the last verse implies that the poem goes beyond its now very evident limitations. The poetic voice says that as soon as one says *it is real,* the words *it is real* dissipate. "Is it more real this way?" can now be seen as a rhetorical question. For the textual *process* continues reconstituting itself and thus continually reaffirms its own self-aware reality.

That the poem is, indeed, now *more* real—a difficult thing to demonstrate convincingly—is in fact the topic of the second poem in this set of two.

Idea palpable,
               palabra
impalpable:
          la poesía
va y viene
          entre lo que es
y lo que no es.
               Teje reflejos
y los desteje.
               La poesía

siembra ojos en la página,
siembra palabras en los ojos.
Los ojos hablan,
                    las palabras miran,
las miradas piensan.
                              Oír
los pensamientos,
                    ver
lo que decimos,
                    tocar
el cuerpo de la idea.
                              Los ojos
se cierran,
          las palabras se abren.

                                        (12–13)

[Touchable idea,
          untouchable
word.
               Poetry
comes and goes
          between what is
and what is not.
          It weaves reflections
and unweaves them.
                    Poetry
sows eyes on the page
it sows words on the eyes.
The eyes speak,
          the words look,
the looks think.
                              Hearing
thoughts,
                    seeing
what we say,
                    touching
the body of the idea.
                    Eyes
shut,
          words open.]

Seen in terms of contradictions—palpable/impalpable, what is/
what is not—this poetic text and the poetry it describes show what
the critical poem must be and do. In *The Bow and the Lyre* Paz
says that "since Parmenides our world has been the world of clear
and trenchant distinctions between what is and what is not"—

exactly the chief distinction that is key to this poem. But, says Paz, the critical poem "not only proclaims the dynamic and necessary coexistence of opposites, but also their ultimate identity" (a concept already integral to Oriental thought, he also points out) (86–87). Shuttling between the extremes, this text takes on the characteristics of a loom, with the rapid rhythm of the brief lines (like a weaver rapidly moving the shuttle back and forth) and the image of weaving and unweaving. The poem's texture is thus characterized by the tension produced between these opposing elements, but that tension then produces its own dynamic activity: poetry here *sows* words and eyes, which in turn become active: eyes speak, words look, glances think, resulting in a reversal of sensory expectations—a type of synesthesia. The final image, of eyes closing and words opening, now has a double purpose. It shows the importance of the reader to the text's ability to produce a dynamic result, and it also shows how the word, now viewed critically and with its opposing tensions revealed, effectively opens up new possibilities. This text can thus be seen as a perfect illustration of a definition that Paz gives of the poetic word, also in *The Bow and the Lyre*: "An ambivalent being, the poetic word is completely that which it is—rhythm, color meaning—and it is something else: image. . . . This second quality, that of being images, and the strange power they have to arouse in the listener or spectator constellations of images, turns all works of art into poems (12)."

In the second poem to Jakobson, above, the words do indeed create images, as we saw. The poem becomes an image of a poetic text as an actively woven tapestry that operates in turn in a tension between presence and absence, words and thoughts. It is clear that both of these poems perfectly illustrate just what a critical poem must be. In each case the poetic text demonstrates an acute awareness of what it is—that it depends on revelations of its own fallibilities to create, and continually recreate, its true texture, constellations of shimmering images: "it weaves *reflections* and unweaves them."

3

Roberto Juarroz: Exploding the Limits

Like Octavio Paz, whom he admired as a "thinker about what is poetic," Roberto Juarroz revealed his concern with language and its problems in his first published poems. Unlike Paz, however, for whom language was only one of several recurring themes, Juarroz focused almost entirely on language in his poetry.

Intensely withdrawn as a person and a deeply philosophical thinker, this professor of library science (Argentina, 1925–95) at the University of Buenos Aires would not seem typecast as a proponent of something he has called "explosive poetry." But his early awareness of the restrictions inherent in conventional views of language led him, he has said, to a "poetry of limits, which is what interests me."[1] His goal, of course, was somehow to go beyond those limits. The desire to exceed the limits of poetry, paradoxically, also led Juarroz to impose what look like severe limitations on his own work. There could be no better symbol of his rigorous self-restriction than the fact that all of his collections of poetry have had the same title, *Poesía vertical*—from the first in 1958 to the latest, the (eleventh) *Undécima poesía vertical*.

From the beginning, Juarroz's texts were single-mindedly introspective, focusing on the poetic process; there has been no more consistent practitioner of the critical poem. In fact, almost as if he were expanding on Octavio Paz's commentaries of what a critical poem must be, Juarroz made the following observations in one of several interviews that he had with the poet Guillermo Boido in the late 1970s: "I have thought that poetry ought to arrive at what is unsayable. . . . This brings me to the idea of a metapoetry, of a metapoem. A metapoetry as a creative counterproposal, inventive, imaginative rather than rational . . ."[2] Metapoetry is just what Juarroz's poetry is, even with the first *Poesía vertical* in 1958. Poetry that points out its own impossibilities, this "vertical poetry" also prefigures and parallels ideas central to poststructuralist literary theory. This is something we will be seeing throughout this study:

51

how the critical poets seem to reflect or put into practice important developments in (mainly French) literary theory. We should make clear, though, that Juarroz, like Borges before him (and Borges's influence on the major figures in French poststructuralism is legendary), followed his own lead. As is the case with Borges's work, "vertical poetry"—and all it encompasses—predates the work of almost all of the poststructuralist thinkers. Both Juarroz and Borges also manage to reduce demanding philosophical topics into concise and gripping texts, in stark contrast to the heavy prose of the theoreticians. But since there are such uncanny similarities between some of Juarroz's poems and the philosophical and theoretical writings of Jacques Derrida and Maurice Blanchot, in particular, it seems worthwhile to point them out. Weaving some useful statements by these influential French thinkers into our analysis of Juarroz's poems should also help clarify some of the rather difficult concepts they explore.

The idea of "exploring" usually connotes going outside or beyond established territory: exploring the North American frontier during the last century or perhaps exploring outer space. Juarroz's explorations are turned inward. At first, it might seem that a poetry preoccupied by its own limits and then turned in on itself would be both static and stagnant. However, since Octavio Paz's explanations of the critical poem have already shown us how a text can overcome its limits by undoing or undermining itself, we can't be too surprised that even in the first *Poesía vertical,* Juarroz's texts reveal a clear optimism. Here, for example, are some verses that energetically point to new beginnings:

> Sí hay un fondo.

> Pero, es el lugar donde empieza el otro lado,
> simétrico de éste,
> tal vez éste repetido,
> tal vez éste y su doble,
> tal vez éste.[3]

> [Yes, there is a bottom.

> But, it's the place where the other side begins,
> symmetrical with this one,
> maybe this one repeated,
> maybe this one and its double,
> maybe this one.]

We have here a synthesis of the search for a basis for poetry that Juarroz carries out in his series of vertical poetries. This search depends on two crucial and interdependent elements. The first is the quest for a center ("it's the place where the other side begins"), which is the main concern in many of these poems. The second is the constant need for repetition, a hallmark in Juarroz's poetry. Guillermo Sucre, regarding Juarroz's obsession with repetition, says, "His is a discourse that incessantly repeats itself"; and W. S. Merwin, a superb translator of Juarroz into English, has even said (at a 1981 reading) that "Juarroz is too repetitive at times." In the lines cited above, repetition is indicated by the words "repetido," "doble," "simétrico" (repeated, double, symmetrical) and the anaphora of "tal vez éste" (perhaps this one). These two constants—the center and repetition—determine the investigation into the problem of structure, one of Juarroz's most important themes. It is precisely this concern with structure that precedes, and then later parallels, the similar but more philosophical concerns of Jacques Derrida. Derrida makes clear, however, that this is not a "structuralist"—as in the theoretical movement—concern, but rather a new way of looking at the historical concept of structure itself. The key to this concept is, as it is in Juarroz's poetry, the process of repetition. A review of some of Derrida's reflections in "Structure, Sign and Play" will help us to understand the similar explorations that we see in Juarroz:

> Perhaps there is produced in the history of the concept of structure something that one could call an "event" if that word did not carry with it a load of meaning that structural—or structuralist—exigency rightly has as a function of reducing or suspecting. Nevertheless, we will say an "event" and we will use the word, cautiously, between quotation marks. What would this event be, then? It would have the exterior form of a *rupture* and a redoubling.[4]

This *redoubling* for Derrida is the result of a self-reflection—within the work—of its own "structurality." Juarroz's poem illustrated that very phenomenon and said it better ("it's the place where the other side begins, symmetrical to this one"). Derrida further clarifies this idea when he explains what he understands by "event": "The event of rupture, the disruption to which I alluded at the beginning, would perhaps be produced at the moment where the structure ought to begin to be thought of, that is to say, repeated."

For Juarroz, as for Derrida, the central element of "the structurality of the structure," and, by extension, of the essential repetition, is the search for the "center." As a matter of fact, the insecurity or the ambiguity of the center is what makes repetition so necessary and, at the same time, so valuable. The importance of this search is something that Derrida explains in more detail in the same essay: "One has thus always thought that the center, which by definition is unique, made up, in a structure, that very thing that, in control of the structure, escapes from the structurality. This is why, for a classical idea of the structure, the center can be said to be, paradoxically, *in* the structure and *outside of* the structure." Juarroz prefigures that same observation when he does not hesitate to declare, more succinctly, in his poem 16 in the second *Poesía vertical* (1963), how difficult this search for a center is.

> El centro no es un punto,
> Si lo fuera, resultaría fácil acertarlo.

(73)

> [The center is not a point,
> if it were, it would be hard to ascertain it.]

Almost as if he wanted to show that he is speaking of the same center that is the point of this poem, Derrida goes a bit beyond that concept of "the center is not a point" when he says that "the center is not the center." What Derrida is driving at is that with each new structure (a word, a poem, whatever) there is a new center ("a series of substitutions from center to center, a chain of determinations of the center"). A perfect example of this idea in a Juarroz text is found in poem 2 from the tenth *Poesía vertical* (1986):

> Pero ningún signo o palabra
> vuelve nunca a su sitio
>
> . . . .
>
> Tal vez por eso
> cada palabra o signo
> debe volver a nacer constantemente en otra parte.
> El lugar de una palabra
> es siempre otro.[5]
>
> [But no word or sign
> ever returns to its place
>
> . . . .
>
> Perhaps for that reason

each word or sign
ought to be constantly born again somewhere else.
The place of each word
is always another place.]

With each new context that it finds itself in, the word is "constantly born again somewhere else." This is because each word or sign, when it is repeated, belongs to a changed or different structure that has a new—or displaced—center. This shift, causing a change or deferral in meaning, is approximately what Derrida means by his term "différance" (his neologism, as we noted previously, which combines the French words for "differ" and "defer"). Now, with the addition of each new repetition of a word, the center of the whole poetic construction is displaced yet again. This whole process thus creates a series of new "centers" by means of "infinite substitutions," says Derrida. In addition, new textual activity comes out of the process that he calls "supplémentarité": the sign that replaces the displaced center supplements it ("en supplément") and adds something ("ajoute quelque chose"). He also explains that it is the capacity of the center to be simultaneously inside and "*outside of* the structure" (his emphasis) that allows this movement and this infinite repetition of the structure. Further clarification of the function of this new concept of the "center" comes from Maurice Blanchot, for whom the center becomes "the concentration of ambiguity," and the poetic word that comes out of this process becomes "a neutral word," which he describes this way:

> This word is essentially a wandering one, being always outside of itself. It designates the infinitely distended outside that has its place in the intimacy of the word. It resembles the echo, when the echo not only says what is at first murmured, but is confused with the whispering immensity; it is silence become retaining space, the outside of every word. Only, here, the outside is empty, and the echo repeats in advance, "prophetic in the absence of time."[6]

The idea of a changing or ambiguous center is a theme that reappears constantly in Juarroz's poetry. In fact, this idea of a shifting center leads to a concept of the "poetic sign," which is almost a perfect "echo" of the echo in Blanchot's own text. It also calls to mind the Idealist dilemma—if a tree falls in the middle of the forest, with no one to hear it, does it make a sound? Here, for example, is a verse from a Juarroz poem:

Hasta el tronco central cae afuera del bosque.

(123)

[Even the central trunk falls outside of the forest.]

In Juarroz's poems 52 (from 1963) and 8 (from 1965) we find graphic explanations of the process of structural repetition in—or around—a changing center.

Si alguien
cayendo de sí mismo en sí mismo,
manotea para sostener de sí
y encuentra entre él y él
una puerta que lleva a otra parte,
feliz de él y de él,
pues ha encontrado su borrador más antiguo,
la primera copia.

(94)

[If someone
falling from himself into himself,
flaps his arms to stay up
and finds between himself and himself
a door that leads to somewhere else,
happy with himself and himself,
then he has found his oldest rough draft,
the first copy.]

Although it is a kind of allegory expressed in personal terms, referring to "someone," it is clear that the poem deals with the acts of redoubling ("falling from himself to himself") and of repetition by means of simple elements ("between himself and himself") whose capacity of dividing or duplicating and then of repeating themselves (Derrida's "rupture" and "dédoublement") indicates that there is an ambiguous center providing the "someone" with a "door that leads somewhere else." This "somewhere else" can be seen as the beginning of the artistic process, the "first copy" that is still only the "oldest rough draft." This final image is a Borgesian one in which the work of art is seen as a palimpsest: a manuscript composed of many levels of texts, words on top of other displaced words. The metaphor is an apt one for the descriptions that Juarroz gives of the poetic process, which he sees as a continuous development fed by repetitions of words. In poem 8 we see another version of this same procedure:

Hay instantes en que el mundo se contrae,
se aprieta en torno a un punto vivo,
para defender allí una culminación de la densidad,
una flor de raíz,
una letra inicial o final.

(146)

[There are instants in which the world contracts,
it tightens around a living point
to defend there a culmination of density,
a root flower,
a first or final letter.]

Obviously, the "world that contracts" in this poem is yet another
way of displaying the doubling effect in the fall "from himself into
himself" from poem 52, and the "living point" from this poem is
one more description of the "center that is not the center." As
more texts get added to Juarroz's "vertical" poetry, forming a
virtual palimpsest, repetition attains a "culmination of density,"
which has a certain similarity to Derrida's concept of "supplémentarité." As the final two lines indicate, repetition leads, in fact,
to a creative stage, even if the creation may be a bit uncertain. It
is important to note here that these texts leave us with an indefinite
idea about beginnings and endings ("rough draft," "flower/root,"
"first or last"), obviously forming part of Juarroz's rebellion against
limits, something that another poem from 1963 clearly shows:

El signo no es algo que ocurre entre sus extremos
sino la anulación de esos extremos.
Lo que ocurre entre ellos
sucede en verdad afuera.
Promontorio con forma de valle
donde el ojo comprende su sustancia.

(83)

[The sign is not something that happens between its ends
but rather a doing away with those ends.
What happens between them
really takes place outside.
A promontory with the shape of a valley
where the eye understands its substance.]

Here we see how Juarroz's expression of this idea closely coincides with Blanchot's concept that the word "is essentially wandering, being always outside of itself." The first verse of this poem

gives a more explicit version of the separability or the "rupture" of the sign that we saw previously in the "entre él y él" (between him and him) of poem 52. The limits ("los extremos") that are the results of that opening of the sign can be erased ("la anulación de los extremos") by the very concept of the sign that "takes place outside" and that is, in Blanchot's words, "always outside of itself." Given this apparent liberation from any limitations, Juarroz, in another poem, examines "the very limits of what can be named" (103). Because words, at least the ones we use in everyday communication, have their own meanings and are limited by those meanings, as we see in poem 45 from the fourth collection (1969):

> El fruto se rompe
> en el límite mismo de la mano.
> El fruto quiere ser mano y no fruto,
> límite de sí mismo,
> corazón enrollado.

>   (208)

> [The fruit breaks
> at the edges of the hand.
> The fruit wants to be hand and not fruit,
> its own edge,
> a rolled up heart.]

This particular poem goes on with a series of stanzas that follow the same model ("the road breaks," "love breaks," and so on), where the objects named, like the words that represent them, are described as if they were incapable of rising above the circumstances of their own "présence," to use Derrida's term.

The sense of restriction extends from the word to the written page, and then, in poem 2, from 1974, to the creative process itself:

Llega un día
en que la mano percibe los límites de la página
y siente que las sombras de las letras que escribe
saltan del papel.

Detrás de esas sombras,
pasa entonces a escribir en los cuerpos repartidos por el mundo,
en un brazo extendido,
en una copa vacía,
en los restos de algo.

Pero llega otro día
en que la mano siente que todo cuerpo devora
furtiva y precozmente
el oscuro alimento de los signos.

Ha llegado para ella el momento
de escribir en el aire,
de conformarse casi con su gesto.
Pero el aire también es insaciable
y sus límites son oblicuamente estrechos.

La mano emprende entonces su último cambio:
pasa humildemente
a escribir sobre ella misma.

(226)

[A day comes
in which the hand perceives the limits of the page
and feels that the shadows of the letters that it writes
leap off the page.

Behind those shadows,
it then goes on to write on the bodies scattered around the world,
on an outstretched arm,
on an empty cup,
on the remains of something.

But another day comes
in which the hand feels that every body devours
furtively and precociously
the dark food of the signs.

The time has come for it
to write on the air,
to almost be satisfied with its gesture.
But the air is also insatiable
and its limits are obliquely narrow.

The hand then takes on its final change:
it humbly moves on
to write on itself.]

A poem much like this from the first *Poesía vertical,* which I
will discuss in the concluding chapter, has a similar physical image
linked to the process of writing: "I found a man writing on his
bones." Poem 2 here, written sixteen years later, repeats some of

the elements of that earlier one, especially "the hand," which here writes on the "bodies scattered around the world." And at the end of this poem we see almost a repetition of the earlier model: in the first instance, the hand writes on its own shoulder, while here the hand (the poet) writes "on itself." The third and fourth stanzas add something else, however. We see here that the words ("the signs") have neither existence nor meaning ("food") that go beyond themselves. The work itself devours, or absorbs—puts limits on—the signs' "dark food," an image formed by hypallage, which deftly shows the uncertain or changing nature of the sign itself. Its ephemeral character is made clear in the fourth strophe, where the poet, in this allegory, is reduced to writing on the air, and his art is thus reduced to the gesture of writing. Given the fleeting nature of the sign, as evoked in this text, and the fact that even the air, its final context, has limits that are "obliquely narrow," this poem and its images clearly show that the sign cannot be transmitted.

At this point in his critical poems Juarroz is really pointing in a contrary direction to much of "modern" poetry. A crucial element here is that by denying (or at least in refusing to admit) even the existence of the *signifié*, the received sign, these Juarroz texts theoretically make the metaphor almost inconceivable. Derrida explains this process: "The metaphor in general, going from one being [étant] to another, or from one signified to another, authorized by the initial *submission* and the *analogical* displacement of the act of being [l'être] to the being [l'étant]."[7] Continuing along this line of thought, François Rigolot, in an astute study of the relationship between the poetic and the analogical throughout Western tradition, gives a well-established definition of modern poetry: "An already set idea of modern poetic consciousness, which establishes an equation between the analogical and the poetic and measures the success of a poet by his ability to find speaking analogies: the poet as great *syntaxer* of analogy."[8]

The expression "syntaxer of analogy" perfectly fits the Ultraist poetry that preceded Juarroz in Argentina and applies equally to his Surrealist contemporaries there. Although Juarroz in principal rejects the whole basis of those avant-garde movements, at times, as in poem 18 (from 1974), he succumbs to a temptation to imitate them and to "jot down images." In that poem, however, the process ("I go along jotting down images") also becomes an exercise in futility ("the furtive quotient of shadow / the residue of a lightning bolt," and so forth). What comes out of this series of images expressing a complete lack of substantial results is a Mallarméan absence, the white page that is, paradoxically, a return to the beginning: "I'm arriving at the starting point: the word without anyone" (237). This starting point is, ironically of course, a metaphor now for the word as signifier only (*destinateur* with no *destinataire*).

Such a criticism of the traditional concept of language grows into an awareness of a newly revitalized poetic process, a version of the new "song" promised in Octavio Paz's description of the critical poem. Typically Juarroz expresses this new possibility in paradoxical terms—and in the first-person voice—in the sixth *Poesía vertical* (1975):

> He llegado a mis inseguridades definitivas.
> Aquí comienza el territorio
> donde es posible quemar todos los finales
> y crear el propio abismo,
> para desaparecer hacia adentro.
>
> (273)

> [I have arrived at my definitive insecurities.
> Here begins the territory
> where it is possible to burn all the ends
> and create the abyss itself,
> in order to disappear inside.]

Describing the "insecurities" as "definitive" seems like a paradox, but Juarroz, to the contrary, is reaffirming his certainty regarding the indeterminacy of poetry. These texts see poetry as having no fixed base, and for that reason it has no limits either, a situation that comes from the possibility of opening and duplicating the "signs" that poetry is made of. By doing away with the limits or boundaries of those signs ("burning all the ends"), the poet creates "the abyss itself": an infinitely creative situation in which he can disappear. This final verb underlines both the insecurity mentioned at the beginning of the strophe and the infinity or the poetic depths in which the poetic voice (the "I") finds itself, or better yet, in which it can lose itself.

If any doubt remained that the sign, mentioned throughout the *Poesía vertical* series, represents only the signifier, the following poem from the sixth volume explicitly eliminates those doubts:

> 3
> Hay mensajes cuyo destino es la pérdida,
> palabras anteriores o posteriores a su destinatario,
> imágenes que saltan del otro lado de la visión,
> signos que apuntan más arriba o más abajo de su blanco,

señales sin código,
mensajes envueltos por otros mensajes,
gestos que chocan contra la pared,
un perfume que retrocede sin volver a encontrar su origen,
una música que se vuelca sobre sí misma
como un caracol definitivamente abandonado.

Pero toda pérdida es el pretexto de un hallazgo.
Los mensajes perdidos
inventan siempre a quien debe encontrarlos.

(274)

[There are messages whose fate is to be lost,
words anterior or posterior to their *destinataire,*
images that leap from the other side of vision,
signs that point above or below their target,
signals without a code,
messages wrapped in other messages,
gestures that bump against the wall
a perfume that recedes without returning to find its origin,
a music that overturns on itself
like a definitively abandoned snail shell.

But every loss is an opportunity for a discovery.
The lost messages
always invent the person who should find them.]

The first part of this poem deals with the poetic word ("message," "words," "images," "signs," "signals," "gestures"), as if it had only one aspect or facet, like a signifier without a signified. Even though it may seem tedious to go through all the examples that we find in the poem, it seems worthwhile to underline the explicit way that Juarroz illustrates this central concern of his. In the first two verses, both the destination and *destinataire* are lost. Then there are images that escape from view, badly aimed signs, undecipherable signs, messages held in by other messages, gestures with no way out, an evaporated perfume, a poured-out music, and an abandoned snail shell. But the gospel according to Juarroz says that to have no way out, or to be lost, is exactly like "definitively" finding oneself. "The lost message," that is, the sign as signifier stripped of its signified, now has the power to "invent" or create—by means of an incessant ("always") and autonomous process—its own destination and its own reader, as we learn at the end of the poem.

The same words, as a matter of fact, in poem 31 from 1975, do indeed determine their own destination by "teaching" the poet (the first-person "subject" in the poem) their "secret and solitary rhythm":

> El material con que se construyen las palabras
> y la argamasa que lo une
> me han ido enseñando poco a poco
> un ritmo secreto y solitario.

(294)

> [The material with which words are constructed
> and the clay that holds it together
> have been slowly teaching me
> a secret and solitary rhythm.]

The words' independence stands out clearly in the first line: the words "are constructed" and their components—their material, their clay—take on the task of revealing to the poet the secret rhythm of poetic construction. This whole process, of course, as Blanchot pointed out in detail, goes back to Mallarmé's wish that words would be autonomous so that he could "céder l'initiative aux mots" (let the words have their own initiative). The result of that self-construction is "a music" ("I have thus learned that every construction is music"), reminiscent of the "dissonance that sings" in poem 18. In order to accept that definition of the poetic word, Juarroz has had to make a sacrifice, one that Rigolot would call a "choix réductif poétique" (poetic reductive choice), as we see summarized at the beginning of another important poem, number 40 from the sixth collection (1975). This reduction is characterized by an "unbaptizing of the world" by sacrificing "the *name* of things" (my emphasis). This process of unnaming takes for granted the abandonment of any meaning that the presumed or accepted relationship between signifier and signified might give to the word.

> Desbautizar el mundo,
> sacrificar el nombre de las cosas
> para ganar su presencia.
>
> El mundo es un llamado desnudo,
> una voz y no un nombre,
> una voz con su propio eco a cuestas.
>
> Y la palabra del hombre es una parte de esa voz.
> no una señal con el dedo,
> ni un rótulo de archivo,

ni un perfil de diccionario,
ni una cédula de identidad sonora,
ni un banderín indicativo
de la topografía del abismo.

El oficio de la palabra,
más allá de la pequeña miseria
y la pequeña ternura de designar esto o aquello,
es un acto de amor: crear presencia.

El oficio de la palabra,
es la posibilidad de que el mundo diga al mundo,
la posibilidad de que el mundo diga al hombre.

        La palabra: ese cuerpo hacia todo.
        La palabra: esos ojos abiertos.

                                        (299)

[Debaptize the world,
sacrifice the name of things
to gain their presence.

The world is a naked cry,
a voice and not a name,
a voice with its own echo on its back.

And man's word is a part of that voice,
not a finger pointing,
nor a filing label
nor a dictionary definition,
nor a noisy identification card,
nor a direction flag
for the topography of the abyss.

The word's job,
beyond the small misery
and the small tenderness of designating this or that,
is an act of love: to create presence.

The word's job
is the possibility that the world might say to the world,
the possibility that the word might speak to man.

        The word: that body toward everything.
        The word: those open eyes.]

It is obvious that this poem is both a synthesis and a repetition of key aspects of Juarroz's poetics. That it establishes a poetics based on repetition, in fact, can be seen in the numerous redoublings of words in the poem: "world," "name," "presence," "voice," "word," "man," "job," "possibility." The first stanza, once again, describes the abandonment of the "name of things" (the sign as Signifier/signified). The "naked cry" in the second stanza, like the "voice and not a name," indicates the *destinateur* without a *destinataire*. Continuing this same idea, when the sign emits a resonant and significant "echo," that resonance continues to be a part of the sign: it is not transmitted. The phrase showing that the "echo" belongs to its own body—"on its back"—also carries with it the aspect of "verticality" that Juarroz sees in all the infinitely repeated and repeatable words and structures in his poetic depths: creating a picture of signs, or resonances of signs, on top of each other. The terms "echo" and "on its back" are parallels to the ones Blanchot uses in the previous quotation and in the sentence where he describes writing as an infinite and incessant language. "To write is to make an echo of what cannot stop speaking."[9] As the third stanza of the poem reiterates, the word described in that way does not contain a fixed meaning, a signified, that can be transmitted. It is not "a pointing finger," "a filing label," or any of the other signs in that list.

In the fourth stanza there is a Borgesian type of realization—in the face of reality—that the word does designate "this or that." Its true mission, the poetic mission—which is also, significantly, an act of love—is that of "creating presence." This is, essentially, what Derrida, using the same term, expresses as "the determination of the act of being as presence in all senses of the word." "The act of being" (*l'être*) for Derrida is the term for the signifier, in contrast to "the being" (*l'étant*) for the signified. After rejecting the bipartite structure of the word as Signifier/signified in the first three stanzas, Juarroz now sees a real significance created by the word's act of being (*l'être* in French or *ser* in Spanish). This results in its *presence* as signifier, what Juarroz has called an "explosión del ser" (explosion of being) in describing the poetic process (*Poesía y creación*, 137). The word, thought of in this way, has a clear communicative function in this poetics ("que diga"), which comes from its challenging presence ("its body toward everything") and its inherent possibilities of creation ("those open eyes").

Not only is this poem a repetition and a synthesis of the poetics and the concept of a poetic language that Juarroz has been elaborating; it is also almost a reiteration of Blanchot's idea of the writer and that writer's language. "The writer belongs to a language that no one speaks, which is addressed to no one, which has no center, which reveals nothing. . . . There, where it is, only the act of being [*l'être*] speaks—which signifies that the word speaks no more, but it is, but it avows the pure passivity of the act of being."[10]

When Juarroz, like Blanchot, lets go of the language that "speaks," and in exchange counts on the word as "être" or as signifier only, he is rejecting the search for infinite analogies based on relationships between signifieds, which "modern" poets, beginning with the Symbolists, considered essential. Octavio Paz, in an essay describing the role of analogy in modern poetry since Baudelaire, says that, for the modern poet, the only alternative is an ironic stance. For this modern poet, in fact, Paz says that "irony is not a word, nor a discourse, but rather the other side of the word, a noncommunication."[11]

As we saw in the first two chapters, Paz can say a lot in a few words and does so here. The "noncommunication" is a shorthand way of referring to the departure from the traditional concept of the sign. The ironic stance that the critical poet must take is something that we have not discussed yet. Given Paz's definition of the critical poem, with the poet presiding over a text that negates its own foundations, an ironic approach is almost a necessity. Jorge Rodríguez Padrón explains succinctly and with his own irony how this applies to Juarroz: "In his texts are summarized in an admirable way the power and the poverty of language: the joyful uncertainty of revelation and the discredited evidence of the result. And I say that all of it shows a substantive irony because Juarroz writes from the absolute knowledge of those limitations."[12]

Juarroz himself explains that there is yet another element that the self-aware writer needs in order to continue writing, and in the process he clearly expresses how well he senses the role Paz assigns to the *critical* poet: "And among the things that people can do, and in this sense not do, it seems to me that few are as transcendent, as defining of the human being, as carrying the word to its limits, to its final possibility of configuring, creating, or expressing something. There is behind all this a very deep act of faith" (*Poesía y creación*, 81).

Since carrying the word to its limits has meant a denial of its ability to transmit a fixed message, the poet is left with an obvious dilemma. If an ironic view of this dilemma is one necessary approach to this philosophical and creative problem for the writer, so is the pure leap of faith that Juarroz suggests here. Without making too much of an issue of it, it is nevertheless important to note the parallel with Søren Kierkegaard's theology on this point. For the Danish theologian, a religious person will never truly be able to overcome inevitable doubts of God's existence and at some point will simply have to make a willful decision to act on faith alone. For our critical poets, especially if they see the act of writing as an ethical one, as Juarroz does, a decision to continue writing in the face of a language that poses grave problems requires the same kind of suspension of disbelief, a "leap of faith."

Juarroz, from the beginning, has opted to act on faith as he pursues what we have also seen him call an "act of love": exploring words and their limits. Now, to conclude, here are three recent Juarroz texts illustrating that exploration. The first brilliantly portrays the explosive result of "carrying the word to its limits." The second demonstrates the act of faith that all critical poets will need. And the final one gives us a much more personal view of how this whole critical process has a place in our own development as thoughtful people.

The first of these texts, from the ninth *Poesía vertical* (1986), is a fairly lengthy poem for Juarroz, but since it serves as a fine summary of both his concept of "poesía explosiva" and the paradox it entails, it is worth looking at in its entirety.

> La palabra que llega
> como un proyectil envuelto en terco terciopelo
> y estalla al ponerse en contacto
> con la espera del hombre,
> revela la explosiva epifanía
> que se agazapa como un resorte visionario
> en el núcleo de todas las cosas.
>
> La palabra que estalla
> puede emerger del centro del lenguaje,
> como un ángel verbal
> que de pronto se convierte en demonio.
> Puede venir del fondo del silencio,
> vistiendo solamente
> la piel de la locura más callada.
> Puede brotar de un texto que da vueltas
> adentro de la tómbola del mundo
> con la amenaza impar que es todo texto.
> Puede surgir del hueco de otro hombre,
> de su boca o su sombra,
> como un seco rebote del abismo.

Pero cualquiera sea su origen,
algo salta a la luz en la grieta del golpe:
todo tiende a mostrarse,
a estallar, a expandirse,
a volcarse en lo abierto,
a volverse visible.

La realidad es apofántica,
lo oculto necesita derramarse,
lo cerrado se abre
como un círculo mágico.
Y la palabra es su conjuro,
pero sólo la palabra más sola,
la palabra como un proyectil forrado en tiempo,
la palabra que al final se destruye
en su propio estallido.[13]

[The word that comes
like a projectile wrapped in stubborn velvet
and explodes when it comes in contact
with man's hopes,
reveals the explosive epiphany
which crouches like a visionary spring
in the nucleus of every thing.

The word that explodes
can come from the center of language,
like a verbal angel
that suddenly becomes a demon.
It can come from the depths of silence,
wearing only
the skin of the most toned-down madness.
It can spring from a text that spins
within the tombola of the world
with the odd threat that all texts are.
It can come out of the emptiness of another man,
from his mouth or his shadow,
like a dry rebound from the abyss.

But whatever its origin,
something comes to light in the cracks of the explosion:
everything tends to be displayed,
to explode, to expand,
to throw itself into the open,
to become visible.

Reality is apophantic,
what is hidden needs to overflow,
what is closed opens up
like a magic circle.
And the word calls it into being,
but only the word most alone,
the word like a projectile lined with time,
the word that at the end is destroyed
in its own explosion.]

Here we see what *can* happen through language and poetry, what both poet and reader can hope to experience. It will be both magnificent and powerful. Explosive terms fill the whole poem: "projectile," "explosive," "explodes," "springs," "to explode," "explosion." The first stanza explains enthusiastically how this experience occurs. The word is compared to a projectile launched at human consciousness (man's hopes) and then exploding with evocations of everything the world contains. Then the explosive word is seen as a verbal devil-angel that can come out of either silence or the center of language—paralleling all the contradictory and even self-negating elements that the critical poets view as permeating language. But the word *is* exploding here, it is springing up, coming out of this confusing process.

Whatever its origin, however, as the third section begins, the explosion occurs ("el golpe"), and then all sorts of things break loose: everything spills out, explodes, pours out, becomes visible. Then the last strophe, confusing at first, really summarizes this explosive process. The first line contains an important, if frustrating, idea that explains all the contradictions. "Reality is apophantic" means that reality is hidden *and* revealed. But poetry can be a magical process, in which, as the text says again, the word is the key to conjuring up both what is hidden and what needs to be perceived. It can only be an isolated word, however: one that has no links to set meanings or expectations. And, when its work is finished, when the magical explosive process is over, we see that the word had to be destroyed as part of that experience. The word has had its particular, explosive, and magical effect in this one instance—the word as signifier only, whose particular effect can never be repeated in the same way again. As a result, the poetic process will be an individual experience for each person affected by the words that explode, that work in those magical instances.

Given the vicissitudes that surround the possibilities of this kind of magical collision between word and reader's field of expectations, the excited tone of the poem is bound to give way to the

more ascetic verse usually associated with Juarroz. Even when
the sense of frustration with the verbal process seems to overwhelm such a *poesía vertical,* however, we come upon other positive, if resigned, poems. Here are some lines from Juarroz's
eleventh volume that demonstrate not only the faith that he has
said is necessary, but also a determination to continue in the face
of the most difficult problems confronting poetic creation:

> Hay que proseguir el ensayo.
>
> . . . .
> Aunque la voz del hombre
> esté llena de huecos
> o tal vez sea un hueco,
> hay que proseguir el ensayo.[14]

> [We have to keep on making the effort.
>
> . . . .
> Even though man's voice
> may be full of holes
> or perhaps it is a hole,
> we have to keep on making the effort.]

The need to keep on trying, in spite of the obstacles placed in
the path of contemporary literature by heightened critical awareness, is made clear in the last poem of Juarroz's most recent *poesía
vertical.* This deep, and deeply moving, poem takes the critical
elements we have seen being applied to language, and applies them
to the human condition.

> Toda palabra es una duda,
> todo silencio es otra duda.
> Sin embargo,
> el enlace de ambas
> nos permite respirar.

> Todo dormir es un hundimiento,
> todo despertar es otro hundimiento.
> Sin embargo,
> el enlace de ambos
> nos permite levantarnos otra vez.

> Toda vida es una forma de desvanecerse,
> toda muerte es otra forma.
> Sin embargo,
> el enlace de ambas
> nos permite ser un signo en el vacío.[15]

[Every word is a doubt,
every silence is another doubt.
Nevertheless,
the intertwining of both
allows us to breathe.

All sleeping is a sinking,
all waking is another sinking.
Nevertheless,
the intertwining of both
allows us to get up once again.

All life is a form of vanishing,
all death is another form.
Nevertheless,
the intertwining of both
allows us to be a sign in the void.]

The interplay of opposites in these almost identically structured stanzas begins with what we now see as a summary of the post-structuralist concept of language, described here as a result of the word given presence by its absence (silence). This same interplay then applies to the most mundane activities of our human existence—sleeping and waking, opposing functions that are both compared to sinking or drowning. This is either a cynical look at the sleeping-waking cycle or a humorous one, or perhaps a little of both. Going to sleep does seem to be a kind of sinking into oblivion, but waking up to a new day usually is associated with new beginnings, new possibilities. To see the beginning of a new day as just sinking into new depths may look cynical, but this verse could just be a reference to the way some of us feel for the first hour or so after the alarm goes off. In any case, as the last verse of this stanza indicates, the combination of the two activities—sleeping and waking—does set us in motion again and allow us to "keep on trying."

The final stanza takes us to the essence of life itself. It is not original, of course, to see life and death—each the absence of the other—as interdependent. But this concept, incorporating the interplay of presence and absence, also mirrors the theory of language that underlies the critical poem.

In fact, it is precisely the emphasis on that interplay, the repeated "intertwining" of opposites, that is crucial—crucial to the concept of "explosive" poetry and also, if we can interpose the work of a French philosopher one last time here, crucial to Derrida's theory. This repetition of the word "intertwining" and the interplay between opposites illustrates the process of "re-inscription" that Jeffrey Nealon sees as an overlooked element of Derrida's work. Rather than canceling themselves out, the opposing elements in the text, for Derrida, "must be reinserted in a system that rejects separation, that stands in a discontinuous, withdrawing ground."[16] Instead of trying to state anything definitively, Derrida's continual reinscription, like Juarroz's penchant for repetition, "sets reading in motion," as Nealon would put it. In fact, that is just what happens in the Juarroz poem above. The last line in each of the three stanzas emphasizes that the intertwining of opposites in each puts things into action: allowing for breathing (giving life), for getting up, for being "a sign in the void." Although presented in personal terms—the intertwining of opposites "allows us" to breathe, get up, and be a sign—the interplaying opposites present more than an encouraging and affecting metaphysics. There are a lot of negatives here—doubt, silence, sinking, vanishing—yet overriding them is a constant tension between the opposing terms of life and deatl.. It is precisely that tension that gives meaning to human existence and permits us to make something of it, to be that "sign in the void." In terms of the critical poem, the "intertwinings" or reinscriptions enable the text to stretch beyond the limits of the opposites that play against each other. It is the resulting "withdrawing ground"—of limits that bend, stretch, or dissolve—that lets Juarroz's poetry "explode."

The continued commitment to thinking through the complexities that lie behind this explosive approach to language characterizes Juarroz's ethical imperative. For another "ethical" approach to critical poetry that rivals that of Juarroz in the intensity of its vision, we can turn to the work of the Chilean Juan Luis Martínez. Although both see poetry as a starkly critical process, their texts differ markedly. In fact, Martínez, as we will see, has created a unique book that can be seen as a beautiful, if esoteric, demonstration of critical poetry.

4

The New Novel by Juan Luis Martínez

F OR a pure demonstration of the problems, ideas, and theories underlying the critical poem, we will now consider—as unlikely as it may seem—a book called *La nueva novela* by the Chilean Juan Luis Martínez (1942–93).[1] In spite of its title, this is a resolutely unclassifiable book, especially in generic terms. According to the title it ought to be a novel. To be sure, it does investigate the problems of the implicit author and reader, which would usually be thought of as critical issues of narratology. But the title does throw us off almost immediately. Rudolf Arnheim, discussing how we perceive different works of art, says that genres "have their own implicit rules and therefore arouse different expectations."[2] So here we are, with something called a "novel," expecting a long work of prose fiction, and we are confronted by, among other things, photographs, equations, graphs, collages, and even actual objects. On the page titled "Ichthys" there are two real, metal fishhooks stuck to the page with Scotch tape. Rather than a long prose work, then, this book, with its eclecticism and its chaotic inclusion of diverse topics and themes, looks more like a work of modern art. In the best sense of the term, it is that.

Santiago Daydí-Tolson points in this direction when he calls the book both a "poetic object" and an "esthetic object."[3] It is not, he says, much different from a "montage" or a "collage," common types of plastic art. As such, this unusual book lends itself to a variety of readings—at least as many as allowed by "an exhibit of contemporary art that combined plastic and verbal material." That is an understatement, as I hope to be showing. The number of possible readings is infinite. But Daydí-Tolson correctly implies that *La nueva novela* can be approached from multiple perspectives. One of these, certainly, is perception theory, which is concerned with our relationship to images. We usually process what we see without much awareness of what we are doing, and Arnheim says that "only special circumstances make us realize that it takes an intricate process to form an image."[4] This book could easily be considered such a "special circumstance," with its disparate images and even objects given unexpected contexts. To list all the apparent oddities put into this work would essentially require a catalog of the book; they include things such as blank pages, pages with holes in them, and photographs repeated in different contexts. All of these are situated in a way that surprises us and makes us question just what we are seeing and doing. Part of the reason for this surprise, according to Enrique Lihn and Pedro Lastra, has to do with the book's poetics, which refer to "all the arts whose language is not literally decipherable: painting, music."[5] What this unusual book requires, in fact, is that the reader be as open to it as one would be to a piece of unfamiliar music. In a book on comparative aesthetics, Kevin Barry says that what is needed when hearing a new piece of music is "an aesthetic complex enough to include the pleasures of uncertainty in interpretation and of some free subjectivity in response."[6] Martínez's book provides many opportunities to experience these pleasures of uncertainty—a phrase that could well be used to define La nueva novela.

For all the uncertainties La nueva novela confronts us with, essentially it is a poetic work, albeit a model of a "new kind of poetic writing," as Daydí-Tolson aptly defines it. But it has at least one other function: as a treatise, or more precisely as an expression of phenomenology. This text—or, given its diversity, this collection of texts—is an investigation of literary expression and, specifically, of how the word works within a literary context.

If the book's construction is ambitious, so are its themes, which all happen to be of significant interest to contemporary theoreticians of literature: the reader's role and situation, the concept of the author, the makeup of the literary text with all its gaps and blanks, and the way words function.

We have already mentioned how important the reader's role will be. In fact, La nueva novela, beginning with its cover,[7] is a confrontation with the reader, insisting that he take an active role with respect to the pages being read. I refer pointedly to the reader as a "he" in this case, since the person who takes this book in hand must be, or at least become, a "masculine reader" in Alain Robbe-Grillet's terms. I am referring to the French novelist's theoretical book whose title fits well into this discussion: For a New Novel.[8] For Robbe-Grillet's masculine reader, there can be no passivity. When confronted with Martínez's "new novel," the reader, whether actually female or male, must take an active role, as was the case, for example, with almost any nouveau roman or with

Julio Cortázar's 1963 novel *Rayuela*—where the reader has to decide how to work his way through the maze of chapters. Unlike Cortázar's book of fiction, as experimental as that at first seemed, here one sees from the first page that this is not going to be what one would expect from a "novel." The photographs and other graphic elements disorient us, and there is not the slightest hint of a narrative thread. What lies on these pages is rather a mixture of visual objects and short prose texts. Almost certainly disconcerted, the reader cannot simply absorb this variety of textual experiences. The text itself grabs the reader, pushing him not only to think, but also to participate. It insists that the active reader make or complete the book. This is "reader response" in the extreme. Wolfgang Iser, in an essay specifically discussing the "interaction between text and reader," explains how "the phenomenological theory of art" has led him to the following important conclusion—which describes perfectly how this book has to work (if it is going to):

> the literary work has two poles, which we might call the artistic and the aesthetic: the artistic pole is the author's text, and the aesthetic is the realization accomplished by the reader. In view of this polarity, it is clear that the work itself cannot be identical with the text or with its actualization but must be situated somewhere between the two. It must inevitably be virtual in character, as it cannot be reduced to the reality of the text or to the subjectivity of the reader, and it is from this virtuality that it derives its dynamism. As the reader passes through the various perspectives offered by the text, and relates the different views and patterns to one another, he sets the work in motion and so sets himself in motion too.[9]

Actually, each page of this book is an example of how the text compels the reader to respond and thereby put the work into action. Perhaps page 58 would display this phenomenon particularly well. The text consists of the title, "La página siguiente" (The following page); a dedication, "to Henry Arthur Case"; a photo of a bicycle race; and under it the following:

LA DISTANCIA	se aleja	DE NOSOTROS
para	seguir siendo	ella misma

a.   Suponga que los ciclistas que usted observa en la fotografía viajan a una velocidad promedio de 40 Kms./Hr.

b. Calcule cuántos Kms. han recorrido desde el instante que usted tomó este libro.
c. Calcule cuántos Kms. más recorrerán hasta el instante que usted deje u olvide este libro.[10]

[THE DISTANCE   gets farther away   FROM US

in order to   keep being   itself

a. Suppose that the cyclists that you see in the photograph are traveling at an average speed of 40 Kms./Hr.
b. Calculate how many Kms. they have covered from the time you picked up this book.
c. Calculate how many more Kms. they will cover from the moment you set down or forget this book.]

Starting with the title on the page, the reader must take into account his situation with respect to the text. The words, "The following page" startle him into paying attention to the text. At this specific moment, he must focus on this particular page and then decide whether to take the words literally or as a misleading guide, since he would normally assume that he is now reading "this" page. In any case, he must pay attention to the present moment, a situation underlined by the ironic fact that the page that really follows this one is titled "The preceding page." The only real sequence here, given the contradictory titles, must be determined by the reader at any given moment.

The somewhat poetic definition of distance given here makes us aware of being observers and also establishes the perspective of the three problems that follow, each one of which also depends upon, and insists on, the reader's participation. The first problem (a) wants one to make a simple calculation, but it also implies that the reader can imagine the cyclists' movement. Anyone who has done much bicycle riding will realize that, at forty kilometers per hour, these must be quite proficient riders or racers. The second problem (b) requires the reader to establish an image of the racers in his mind, relating it to his reading of the whole text up to this point. The third (c) reinforces this relationship. It makes the reader begin to think of his future relationship with the book. And that further or extended relationship is brought back into the reader's consciousness on the very next (the "preceding") page, which has a photo of the famous leaning tower of Pisa. The third problem on that page reads, "Calculate how many more meters the tower will have leaned and how many more kilometers the cyclists will go until the moment when you will have set down this book and forgotten Henry Arthur Case." Now, when the reader's attention to the text has become further sharpened, he is asked to extend his calculations up to the point when the book will no longer be part of his consciousness. The reader at this point, even without wishing to, must consider his relationship to the text and with the images that he is forming in his mind because of it. It is likely that the reader will also become aware of his phenomenological role in constructing a personal and unique reading of this text.

Martínez, with all of this textual play, is also demonstrating concepts essential to the critical poem, rather than simply theorizing about them. Here, despite the lack of any explanation of what these cyclists represent in this changing context (two pages in uncertain order, problems calling into question both time and consciousness), they can be viewed as illustrations of textual phenomena that we have seen explained in previous chapters. Like the shifting or floating signifiers we have been discussing, the cyclists' influence or effect on the reader changes drastically with each of these new "problems."

Another of the many direct challenges to the reader is found on pages 26 and 27. The first has the title "Tareas de poesía" (Poetry homework), a kind of map, and a dedication "to Alejandra Pizarnik" (the Argentine poet who committed suicide at the age of thirty-six in 1972). Then on page 27 we find a magnificent example of intertextuality and of forcing the reader's participation. This page also has a title, "1. *El barco ebrio*" (1. The drunken boat), then comes another problem for the reader to solve, then a portrait divided into a right and a left half, with a poem placed between the two halves of the portrait. The problem is this:

Un barco ebrio cuenta sus recuerdos de viaje. Este barco es usted. Dígalo en la primera persona del singular.

[A drunken boat tells its memories of traveling. This boat is you. Tell it in the first person singular.]

The portrait is of Rimbaud, the author of *Le bateau ivre* (The drunken boat), and the poem is by Alejandra Pizarnik.

—¿Recordar con palabras de este mundo,
que partió de mí,
un barco llevándome?

[Remembering with words from this world,
that a boat carrying me
left from me?]

Once again the reader must think about the command, given in the "problem." And even though the answer is given, the reader must order and evaluate the information given there, as well as think of what he will "tell" in his new role as the drunken boat. Then, besides connecting the portrait with the title and the poem with the dedication to Pizarnik, the reader can think about the two juxtapositions because of the relationship between both of these connections: both poets, Rimbaud and Pizarnik, stopped writing poetry when they were young (Rimbaud simply stopped writing after the age of nineteen, and Pizarnik committed suicide at thirty-six); Rimbaud's title and Pizarnik's poem are about strange boats; and so on.

Forcing the reader to include himself in, or with, the text is a necessary condition for *The New Novel*'s plays on the now well accepted theory of the implied author that Wolfgang Iser appropriated from Wayne Booth. According to Booth and Iser, there is no set idea of the "real" author of the work; the existence of some "author" for the work depends, as does the text itself, on the reader's relationship to that text. In other words, the control over the book no longer derives from the author; rather, it has been taken over by the reader, who makes the text exist within his mind.

This concept of the author having only a tangential connection with the work has its first illustration right away: on the cover of this "new novel." There, under the title, we see this:

~~(JUAN LUIS MARTÍNEZ)~~
~~(JUAN DE DIOS MARTÍNEZ)~~

The parentheses indicate the separation between the "(author)"—because this word is always between parentheses in this text—and the now printed text. The uncertainty of his own name and the fact that the two possibilities are crossed out emphasize his contingent existence (as well as the real [author]'s extreme modesty).[11] Here is another example of this phenomenon: "La locura del (autor)" (The (author)'s madness), on page 92, the first part of which is this:

A. EL OIDO DEL AUTOR

¿Qué escucha cuando escucha
los trágicos   trotes   silenciosos
de un caballito   de madera   desarmado?

[A. THE AUTHOR'S EAR

What does he hear when he hears
the tragic   silent   trots
of a wooden   horse   taken apart?]

His inability to determine, to set down what he feels, and the inevitability of the deconstruction of his future texts are seen in the qualifying words: "tragic," "silent," and "taken apart." And his relationship to the work ends in the abyss of silence in the final section of this page:

C. LA AUSENCIA DE SU OBRA:

El silencio escucha silencio
y repite en   silencio
          lo que escucha que no escucha.

[C. THE ABSENCE OF HIS WORK:

Silence hears silence
and repeats   in silence
            what it hears that it does not hear.]

The dismantled work is reduced to absence and silence, but it insists on the presence of these terms by means of the repetition of the signifiers "silence" and "hears." Here the text—and the (author)—are playing with Mallarmé's two main concerns, absence and silence, which become in turn crucial elements for the "critical poem." Both are seen here as necessary preconditions for the production of any textual presence.

The kind of playing with words found in that text recurs throughout *La nueva novela*. In "El lenguaje" (Language) on page 24, one of several "problems" that Martínez takes from the French poet Jean Tardieu, the reader is given the following three tasks:[12]

Tome una palabra corriente. Póngala bien visible sobre una mesa y descríbala de frente, de perfil y de tres cuartos.
  Repita una palabra tantas veces como sea necesario para volatilizarla. Analice el residuo.
  Encuentre un solo verbo para significar el acto que consiste en beber un vaso de vino blanco con un compañero borgoñón, en el café de Los Dos Chinos, a las seis de la tarde, un día de lluvia, hablando de la no-significación del mundo, sabiendo que acaba usted de encontrarse con

su antiguo profesor de química y mientras cerca de usted una mucha-
cha le dice a su amiga: "¡Sabes cómo hice que le viera la cara a Dios!"

[Take a current word. Make it quite visible on a table and describe it
from the front, in profile, and from a three-quarters view.
    Repeat a word as many times as may be necessary to make it disap-
pear. Analyze the residue.
    Find a single verb to signify the act that consists of drinking a glass
of white wine with a Burgundian friend, in the Los Dos Chinos café,
at six in the afternoon, on a rainy day, talking about the nonsignificance
of the world, knowing that you have just run into your former chemistry
professor, while near you a girl says to her friend: "You know how I
made him see the face of God!"]

The first request asks that we consider the word in its physical,
tangible aspect, in all three dimensions. Now that the word is isolated, the second task makes us conscious of its sound, because
of its being repeated, and, again, because of its apparent fragility.
The third explains well the impossibility of explaining, describing,
or communicating anything directly through language.
    These limitations also provide the basis for a certain kind of
humor, one of this book's most attractive characteristics, and
something that Martínez himself considered an essential element in
his work.[13] We also see this kind of special humor in the ludicrous
exhibition of a "naked" text on pages 29 and 30, which also illustrates, in the most literal sense of that term, the impossibility of
communicating effectively through words. Page 29 contains the
poem "The Poor Wretch," in French. The flip side of that page,
number 30, has for its title what would seem to be a play on Valéry's famous poem, "El cementerio marino" (The sailors' cemetery), but it contains the same "Poor Wretch" poem seen from
behind, backward, and with white letters on a black background.
Right underneath the poem printed backward, as if the words
showed right through the page, there is this caption, "La tumba de
los signos" (The tomb of signs), and then comes this explanation:

Las espaldas del desdichado

Esta página, este lado de la página, anverso o reverso, de sí misma,
nos permite la visión de un poema en su más exacta e inmediata textualidad (sin distancia ni traducción): un poema absolutamente plano,
texto sin otro significado que el de su propia superficie. El dibujo de
los signos desnudos que traspasando el delgado espesor de la página
emergen aquí, invertidos sólo en mera escritura, destruyen cualquier

intento de interpretación respecto a una supuesta: "Profundidad de
la literatura."

[THE WRETCH'S SHOULDERS

This page, this side of the page, back or front, by itself allows us a
vision of a poem in its most exact and immediate textuality (without
distance or translation): an absolutely flat poem, a text with no other
signified than that of its own surface. The form of its letters, the physical body of its words, the thickness of the naked signs that by passing
through the thin thickness of the page emerge here, only inverted into
mere writing, destroy any attempt at interpretation with respect to a
supposed "Literary Depth."]

The "naked" and absolutely flat signs in this physical configura-
tion have, in this example of taking things to a literal extreme, no
"depth." Because the physical illustration of the problem looks so
unusual, with the words seeming to show through the page, it may
seem merely humorous. But it visually represents the dilemma
faced by our critical poets, and is even presented as the graveyard,
or the death, of the sign. The poets can pour signs onto the page,
but they sense an inability to endow them with life, or "meaning,"
and thus are only able to leave their words abandoned on the page,
as these appear to be. What we are seeing, of course, just as we
did in Juarroz's poetry, is the phenomenon of the sign considered
as signifier only—"retirándole . . . al signo uno de sus dos elementos constitutivos: el significado" [taking away one of the sign's
two constitutive elements: the signified], as Lihn and Lastra put
it.[14] Martínez was well aware that he was dealing with the limitations of the sign. "The separation of signifier and signified," he
freely admitted in a rare interview given not long before he died,
has had a great effect on modern art, as well as on his own work.
"Unfortunately," he said, "from a certain point of view, I am a poet
who is a manipulator of signifiers."[15]

Games with signifiers are not limited, in this book, to words,
since there are a good number of drawings, photographs, maps,
collages, and the like scattered throughout. As there are repetitions
of words and concepts, so there are repeated appearances of pho-
tos (of Marx—Karl, not Groucho, although the spirit of the latter
seems to run through the book—as well as of Rimbaud, for example). It even includes, three different times, the same photo of a
girl, with various explanations of how our reception or interpretation of this same photo can change. All of this, of course, plays
with the idea of text as phenomenon, as reality. The book includes,

besides the real fishhooks on one page, other objects, like a real
Chilean flag placed between pages 134 and 135 and a poem in
Chinese placed between pages 96 and 97, as if these "objects"
could communicate something directly to us. Within the context
of this book, nevertheless, these objects become works of art in
the same way as do Marcel Duchamp's "readymades."

Although there are many explicit references to avant-garde art,
and to the Surrealists in particular, the key to this book—and the
chief reason why it must be considered a poetic work—can be
found in the homages to Stéphane Mallarmé scattered through it.
An admitted admirer of this French Symbolist, Martínez said that
"he represents one of the extreme experiments in literature."[16] One
Mallarmé-inspired text in particular, "El cisne troquelado" (The
molded swan), resonates throughout the rest of this ambitious
book. Significantly, this poem is preceded by some anticipatory
pages: the first is transparent and has the title, "La página en
blanco" (The white page), while the next page is completely white
on both sides, thus representing what for Mallarmé was the highest
and most desired state of expression. Now prepared, the reader
encounters the following poem, which we are going to reproduce
by sections.

El cisne troquelado

I

                                                  (la búsqueda)
La página replegada sobre la blancura de sí misma.
La apertura del documento cerrado: (EVOLUTIO LIBRIS).
El pliego / el manuscrito: su texto corregido y su lectura.
La escritura de un signo entre otros signos.
La lectura de unas cifras enrolladas.
La página signada / designada: asignada a la blancura.

[The Molded Swan

I

                                                  (the search)
The page folded over the whiteness of itself.
The opening of the closed document: (EVOLUTIO LIBRIS).
The fold / the manuscript: its corrected text and its reading.
The writing of one sign among other signs.
The reading of some rolled-up figures.
The signed / designated page: assigned to whiteness.]

Obviously these lines deal with the theme of the white page, but they are not simply descriptions of the effect of this pristine page, they also emphasize its significance through repetition. According to Michael Riffaterre, "repetition in itself is a sign."[17] In fact, the entire poem is a semiotic play on the sign and the act of signifying. Repetition—which is seen here in the terms "folded," "of itself," "closed," a "sign *among* other signs," "rolled-up figures"—insists on the significance inherent in this duplicated page, reflected or wrapped in itself. When repeated in this way, the page, as can be seen by the three words that have *the* word in the last line ("*sign*ed / de*sign*ated . . . as*sign*ed"), becomes a *sign* itself. This explains the apparently contradictory concept, "the opening of the closed document," since the folded white page becomes the most significant. And this idea is reinforced, repeated, in the first line of the next section of the poem:

II

                              (el encuentro)
Nombrar / signar / cifrar: el designio inmaculado;
su blancura impoluta: su blancor secreto: su reverso blanco.
La página signada con el número de nadie:
el número o el nombre de cualquiera: (LA ANONIMIA / no nombrada).
El proyecto imposible: la compaginación de la blancura.
La lectura de unos signos diseminados en páginas dispersas.
(La página en Blanco): La Escritura Anónima y Plural:
El demonio de la Analogía: su dominio:
La lectura de un signo entre unos cisnes o a la inversa.

[II

                              (the meeting)
Naming / signing / coding: the immaculate designation;
its unpolluted whiteness: its secret whiteness: its white back.
The page signed with no one's number:
the name or number of anyone: (ANONYMITY) / not named).
The impossible project: the reconciliation of whiteness.
The reading of some signs disseminated on scattered pages.
(The White Page): Anonymous and Plural Writing:
Demon of Analogy: its dominion:
The reading of a sign among some swans or the other way around.]

The four words that refer to the process of signifying ("naming," "signing," "coding," "designation") reaffirm that the page's whiteness, specified by "immaculate," is indeed a sign. Once again there is insistence on the significance of the page devoid of writing, in the repetition of the terms that indicate either its whiteness or its pristine nature ("immaculate," "unpolluted whiteness," "secret whiteness," "white back," "signed with no one's number," "reconciliation of whiteness," "The White Page"). The repeated reference to anonymity also makes us think about this book's insistence that the concept of the author—"the (author)"—is very tenuous indeed and loses validity in the face of a truly open text ("the opening of the closed document"). As in the first part of the poem, the last line indicates the theme, or the semiotic concentration, of the third and last section, with its references to the sign and to swans, whose connection will be explained later.

III
                                        (la locura)
El signo de los signos / el signo de los cisnes.
El troquel con el nombre de cualquiera:
el troquel anónimo de alguno que es ninguno:
"El Anónimo Troquel de la Desdicha":

          SIGNE   CYGNE
Le   blanc de la   Mallarmé
          CYGNE   SIGNE

(Analogía troquelada en anonimia):
el no compaginado nombre de la albura:
la presencia troquelada de unos cisnes: el hueco que dejaron:
la ausencia compaginada en nombre de la albura y su designio:
el designio o el diseño vacío de unos signos:
el revés blanco de una página cualquiera:
la inhalación de su blancura venenosa:
la realidad de la página como ficción de sí misma:
el último canto de ese signo en el revés de la página:
el revés de su canto: la exhalación de su último poema.
(¿Y el signo interrogante de su cuello (?)?:
reflejado en el discurso del agua: (¿): es una errata.

        (¿Swan de Dios?)
(¡Recuerda Jxuan de Dios!): (¡Olvidarás la página!)
y en la suprema identidad de su reverso
no invocarás nombre de hombre o de animal.
en nombre de los otros: tus hermanos!
también el agua borrará tu nombre:
el plumaje anónimo: su nombre tañedor de signos
borroso en su designio
                    borrándose al borde de la página . . .
                                                    (87)

[III

                                        (madness)
The sign of signs / the sign of swans.
The mold with anyone's name:
the anonymous mold of someone who is no one:
"The Anonymous Mold of Unhappiness":

     SIGNE   CYGNE
Le   blanc de la   Mallarmé
     CYGNE   SIGNE

(Analogy molded in anonymity):
the nonreconciled name of whiteness:
the molded presence of some swans: the hole that they left:
the absence reconciled in the name of whiteness and its design:
the intention or the empty design of some signs:
the white reverse side of any page:
the inhalation of its poisonous whiteness:
the reality of the page as fiction about itself:
the last song of that sign on the back side of the page:
the other side of its song: the exhalation of its last poem.
(And the question mark of its neck (?)?:
reflected in the discourse of water: (¿): is an errata).

(Swan of God?)
(Remember Jxuan of God!): (You will forget the page!)
and in the supreme identity of its reverse side
you will not invoke the name of man or animal.
in the name of others: your brothers!
the water will also erase your name:
the anonymous plumage: its name a player of signs

blurry in its design
                erasing itself at the edge of the page. . . .]

In the first verse, the absolute comparative of "the sign of signs,"
and the triple repetition of the term "sign," emphasize the importance of the swans/signs. Seeing these two signs together makes us
immediately think of the relationship that Mallarmé made between
these French homonyms, a relationship that the text makes explicit
in the line set apart. SIGNE (sign) = CYGNE (swan) both as word
and as definitive Sign. And in the text we see why the swan represents the height of signification; it symbolizes the purity of the
magical white page, an idea indicated semiotically through repetition once again in this long list ("name of whiteness", "the hole
that they left," "whiteness and its design," "the empty design of

some signs," "the white reverse side of any page," "anonymous plumage," "blurry in its design," "erasing itself [from] the page"). In addition to all of this whiteness, the word *swan* is repeated five times, once again indicating its own importance as sign. It is also, in a play on words, associated with the (author) eight lines before the end of the poem. The play is on the English word *swan,* of course, and it is a humorous touch to put these other references to the (author) between parentheses also. The insistence that "you will forget the page!" reminds us of the games or problems presented by the author in other parts of the book, and it also has to do with the whiteness and emptiness of the "ideal page," the erased page with which the poem ends. The swan's "erasure" function is also repeated four times in the last three lines ("water will . . . erase," "anonymous plumage," "blurry," "erasing itself"), emphasizing that it can only function as a signifier and cannot transmit anything meaningful—least of all the poetic ideal. The sign of the swan, the question mark, repeated several times, is also another case of intertextuality, since it clearly reminds us of Rubén Darío's poem "Los Cisnes": "¿Qué signo haces, oh cisne, con tu encorvado cuello?" (What sign do you make, O swan, with your curved neck?)

This interrogative function, we should remember, is the most important aspect of Martínez's "new novel." And it is fitting that the swan serve metaphorically as a question mark. The swan, especially for Mallarmé and the Symbolists, was the very emblem of poetic perfection. This poetic text, so central to Martínez's ambitious book, uses that symbol of the ideal as a prime tool for questioning and then undermining, as a critical poem should do, all the traditional assumptions that underlie the quest for that ideal. Finally, the connection with Mallarmé made by the references to the swan and the white page remind us that Martínez is working— throughout *La nueva novela*—from the very same perspective as was Octavio Paz in his essay on "Un coup de dés . . ." But where we saw Paz use his reading of Mallarmé as a key to working out a definition of the "critical poem," in *La nueva novela* we see Martínez use that same source as the focal point of this brilliant, if idiosyncratic, critical text.

The term "idiosyncratic" applies equally well to the next poet, Alejandra Pizarnik. As intense as Juarroz and Martínez in her texts, Pizarnik channels a fascination with death into a deeply philosophical approach to the problems of the critical poem.

5

The Negative Poems of Alejandra Pizarnik

Highly admired throughout Latin America, Alejandra Pizarnik's poetry probably has its greatest popularity with the younger generation. There are several reasons for that appeal to the young audience. Her poems are extremely brief, yet they deal with profound themes—the relations between life and death, presence and absence, language and silence. The tensions that those opposing themes cause in her verse both create and underscore a sense of personal anguish that then burnishes the mystique of Alejandra's tragic death by suicide.

As unlikely as it might seem, Pizarnik's tiny poems, which exert such a strong personal and psychological pull, are at the same time outstanding examples of critical poetry. Underlying all of Pizarnik's verse, as is the case with the other writers we are studying, is a frustration with language, clearly summarized in these two lines from her poem "En esta noche, en este mundo" (In this night, in this world): "Los deterioros de las palabras / deshabitando el palacio del lenguaje" (words' deteriorations / disinhabiting the palace of language).[1] What makes Pizarnik's work so unique is the exquisite construction of her poems, loaded with terms—often negative ones—carrying *both* psychological and philosophical implications. This apparently pessimistic perspective also brings these texts in line with Paz's idea of the critical poem that undermines its own existence. Built around such negative elements as death and absence, or even a concept of negative space, these poems contain, in a dual sense, "their own negation." First, the thematics of the poems, as will be readily apparent, is largely overdetermined by these negative elements. Then, even more important, these same negative terms or concepts form part of a poetic system that criticizes the efficacy of language. This confluence of personal, philosophical, and linguistic negation becomes, finally, the poem's reason for being, "a point of departure for their song," as Paz put it.

87

Inevitably, Pizarnik's biographical data predetermine the way in which we look at her work. An Argentine poet and painter, she died by her own hand—of an overdose of seconal—in 1972 at the age of thirty-six.[2] The circumstances of her death also lead the reader to establish a link with Alfonsina Storni, the other well-known Argentine woman poet who died by suicide. Since the concern here will be to show how her work exemplifies the concept of critical poetry, this study will be neither biographical nor psychological, although those elements will still provide a focus for this semiotic piecing together of what she herself called a fragmented body of writing. The poems themselves are usually very short, sometimes consisting of only two or three lines, which, in turn, are often brief or truncated. In addition, an identifiably surrealist cast helps to give these poems an unfinished and indefinite appearance.

Two central preoccupations, death and absence, run through these poems. But, even though these themes provide a unity for the fragmentary verses, they create difficulties as well, since, as they are used here, they are concepts difficult to grasp. In Pizarnik's texts both death and absence are treated as necessary, desirable factors for poetry and indeed for language itself. A quick look at her biographical information may well help to orient us as readers.[3] Since we know that the poet committed suicide, we can expect a fascination with death as a topic. The concept of absence as a source for poetry is a difficult one, but it is helpful to remember that Pizarnik was also a painter. Painters often say that they start out thinking of the empty canvas as a "negative space," the background or nonoccupied area that determines the painting. Pizarnik looked at her poems precisely in this way, even to the point of hanging them on the walls of her home, as she did her paintings, in order to get a clearer perspective on them.[4]

A reader who is at all aware of those biographical elements is almost sure to look for morbid aspects in Pizarnik's poetry. Death, then, should be the first focal point of our reading, especially since it is so frequently mentioned even in her earliest work. The following brief poem, fragmentary in appearance, is from Pizarnik's second book and shows, even in these three short lines, how death exerts its own presence.

BALADA DE LA PIEDRA QUE LLORA

la muerte se muere de risa pero la vida
se muere de llanto pero la muerte pero la vida
pero nada nada nada[5]

[BALLAD OF THE STONE THAT WEEPS

> death dies from laughing but life
> dies from crying but death but life
> but nothing nothing nothing]

Repetition of the central terms in the poem ("death," "dies," "life," "nothing") forces those elements to the surface. These items, including the process of repetition itself, provide keys to the poetic work she was yet to develop. Death acting on itself ("la muerte se muere") draws attention to itself at the beginning of the poem, but the apparently confused alternation with its opposite ("la vida") leads to an evidently despairing "nada." Setting up two opposites against each other—here a "presence" ("vida") against an "absence" ("muerte")—is a common device in Pizarnik's poetry, even more crucial to her texts than the "intertwining" of opposites that we saw in Juarroz. This is also one of the chief ways in which her work fits into Octavio Paz's conception of critical verse since, as he says in *The Bow and the Lyre,* "now, the poem not only proclaims the dynamic and necessary coexistence of opposites, but also their ultimate identity."[6] In Pizarnik's texts the presence-versus-absence face-off almost always results in a "nada," an apparent victory of absence. But the word "nothing" implies that absence is present; it exists. In any case, rather than annulling the poem that represents this absence, the "nada" is its very reason for being. As Michael Riffaterre explains in his *Semiotics of Poetry,* all poems have a core or nucleus from which they are created. The process of poetic creation, in fact, is a transformation of that matrix, a hypothetical word or minimal sentence, into "a longer, complex, and nonliteral periphrasis."[7] Absence, the "nada nada nada" around which this poem is built, is its "matrix." Besides being the matrix of this poem, "absence" also becomes the central core word of Pizarnik's entire published work; it is, in fact, the "archiseme," or central characteristic, that will "overdetermine" (to use two more of Riffaterre's terms) other, related, elements in her work. This may become a bit more clear if we go back to the earlier comparison between her poetry and her painting. In this context it is easy to see that Pizarnik's poems are similar to what artists refer to as "negative paintings." In those paintings, the artist paints a few colored areas near the middle of the painting, and then fills in the "negative space" all around the colored splotches. In Pizarnik's poems—which almost look like negative paintings with their few short lines in the middle of the page—the concept of absence has this same active and determining function.

However, if absence is the determining characteristic, the obvious question then becomes: what, if anything, does exist? A possible answer, and one that indicates how she is also trying to overcome the restrictions of language, comes in "La noche" (Night) from *Las aventuras perdidas* (1958).

> Tal vez la noche sea la vida y el sol la muerte.
> Tal vez la noche es nada
> y las conjeturas sobre ella nada
> y los seres que la viven nada.
> Tal vez las palabras sean lo único que existe
> en el enorme vacío de los siglos
> que nos arañan el alma con sus recuerdos.[8]

> [Perhaps night is life and the sun is death.
> Perhaps night is nothing
> and conjectures about it are nothing
> and the beings that live it are nothing.
> Perhaps words are the only thing that exist
> in the enormous emptiness of the centuries
> that scratches our souls with its memories.]

In the midst of that pervasive absence ("nada . . . nada . . . nada," again), the text nevertheless implies that there may ("tal vez") exist one thing: words. An insistent repetition of the words that indicate either uncertainty ("tal vez") or absence ("noche" and "nada") illustrates, quite graphically, how Pizarnik uses language to turn her poems into textual representations of the core of absence. So even if words "are the only thing that exist," they can be used to explain absences, as another poem, a complete but fragmentary one from *Arbol de Diana* (1962), shows in an equally graphic way:

> explicar con palabras de este mundo
> que partió de mí un barco llevándome.
>
> (*OC,* 207)

> [explaining with words from this world
> that a ship left from out of me carrying me away.]

Here, however, the absence caused by the carrying away of her own self might be described as an ambivalent one, since she is aware of a "desdoblamiento," which results in a self with two aspects: a self that remains ("de mí") and the self that is carried away ("llevándome"). As the next poem in the same volume makes clear, this awareness of a two-faceted self is a problem that gnaws away at the first-person subject of the poem.

> El poema que no digo,
> el que no merezco.
> Miedo de ser dos
> camino del espejo:
> alguien en mí dormido
> me come y me bebe.
>
> (*OC*, 207)

> [The poem I don't say
> the one I don't deserve.
> Fear of being two
> the mirror's path
> someone asleep within me
> eats and drinks me.]

The play on presence versus absence again pervades this little poem. The *present* text, in fact, evokes, in a Mallarméan way, an *absent* poem: "the one I don't say," a clear echo of Mallarmé's "l'absente de tous bouquets" (the one missing from all bouquets). And it is an absent aspect of her, her lost and nostalgically remembered childhood, that holds a latent control over her ("someone asleep within me") and causes a fear of duplication ("fear of being two"). The duplication here occurs through the reflection of the mirror, a device Pizarnik often uses to represent the double-faceted self. An explanation for this particular fascination comes in a later poem, from 1968:

> He tenido muchos amores—dije—pero el más
> hermoso fue mi amor por los espejos.
>
> (*OC*, 271)

> [I have had many loves—I said—but the most
> beautiful was my love for mirrors.]

The mirror's capability of eternal reduplication helps to justify her preoccupation with a self that is always aware of its other, absent, facet, as we see in another very brief poem:

Delicia de perderse en la imagen presentida. Yo me levanté de mi cadaver, yo fui en busca de quien soy. Peregrina de mí, he ido hacia la que duerme en un país al viento.

(OC, 279)

[Delight in losing herself in the image she could sense. I got up from my cadaver, I went in search of who I am. A pilgrim of myself, I've gone toward the one who sleeps in a country in the wind.]

More than just being aware of a second aspect of the self, we see here that this process of self-reflection is an integral part of the poetic process that these texts are developing—part of the probing into language—and something in which the poetic subject revels. That this desire for an alter ego is a conscious process is clearly drawn in this poem; the verbs indicate a determined action ("me levanté de mí," "yo fui," "he ido"). Equally clear is the necessary connection between that active splitting of the self and the creation of these poems, a relationship that the two key words "image" and "wind" point to. Since the word "viento" (wind) often stands for unlimited poetic expression in Pizarnik's poetry, the final image ("un país al viento") can be seen as a metaphor for the world of poetry. A more explicit statement of the crucial link between her duplicated self and her poetry comes in a key poem from Nombres y figuras (Names and figures) (1969): "no puedo hablar con mi voz sino con mis voces" (I can't speak with my voice, only with my voices) (296). Even though this awareness of duality makes poetry possible, it is an anguished procedure due to the tension produced by the unbridgeable nature of the dualities.

he nacido tanto
y doblemente sufrido
en la memoria de aquí y allá

(OC, 211)

[I have been born so much
and doubly suffered
in the memory of here and there]

The "allá" is her nonpresent self, which in Pizarnik's poetic system is also called "mi otra orilla" (my other shore), or her childhood, as we can see from an early poem from Las aventuras perdidas:

TIEMPO

Yo no sé de la infancia
más que un miedo luminoso
y una mano que me arrastra
a mi otra orilla.

Mi infancia y su perfume
a pájaro acariciado.

(Aventuras, 36)

[TIME

The only thing I know about childhood
is a luminous fear
and a hand that drags me
to my other shore.

My childhood and its perfume
of caressed bird.]

Remembered in the wistful and ethereal image created through the use of synesthesia—"with its perfume of caressed bird"—her childhood is that "allá," the absent past self, now dead to her. As we saw previously, reminiscing about that longed-for past self eats away at her, but Pizarnik's poems also present an inverse way of viewing this basic image of her childhood ("the other shore"), as the absent and dead facet of her self.

Death, too, is seen as both "the other side" and a magical "garden." One example of this "other side" is the poem "Rescate."

RESCATE

Y es siempre el jardín de lilas del otro lado del río.
Si el alma pregunta si queda lejos se le responderá:
del otro lado del río, no éste sino aquél.

(OC, 272)

[RESCUE

And it's always the lilac garden on the other side of the river.
If the soul asks if it's far away the answer is:
on the other side of the river, not this one but that one.]

This lilac garden, the focal point of the dialog between the self and its inner face (the "soul" in this poem), is clearly equated with death. The text emphasizes, again through repetition, that the garden is indeed on "the other side," composed of lilacs, a flower traditionally associated with death, a connection maintained throughout Pizarnik's work. The image of death as a flowering garden convincingly conveys its essential role as inspirational source for her poetry. Even more convincing in this regard is the following short prose poem, part of a series called "Fragmentos para dominar el silencio" (Fragments for dominating silence):

> La muerte ha restituido al silencio su prestigio hechizante. Y yo no diré mi poema y yo he de decirlo. Aun si el poema (aquí, ahora) no tiene sentido, no tiene destino.
>
> (*OC*, 269)

> [Death has restored to silence its enchanting prestige. And I will not say my poem and I must say it. Even if the poem (here, now) has no meaning, has no destination.]

Here we have a clear example of a "critical" poem—which also shows how "death" goes well beyond the personal and psychological level to form a key element in the poetics established in Pizarnik's texts. And all of this is expressed in the barest minimum of words. That brevity, as in the rest of Pizarnik's work, is part of the message, as her texts are always working against the absence of the negative space, the whiteness of the page. The poem begins with death as the active and positive element—the spell that it casts gives value to the silence. This productive silence provides a positive tension that tugs against the clear awareness of a language that does not work, that gives "no meaning" and "no destination" to the poem. That tension, then, as Paz said it would, generates this new critical "song": the middle of these three sentences is a tug ("I will not say," "I must say") between the death/silence that appears in the first sentence and the created poem we find at the end of the text.

Contrary to ordinary expectations, then, it is quite evident by now that death, the "garden," has become a desirable source of creative material in these texts, as the positive terms "heir," "vision," and "forbidden garden" indicate, and which the following paragraph from a key poem from *Nombres y figuras*, "El deseo de la palabra" (Desire for the word), makes all the more clear:

La noche, de nuevo la noche, la magistral sapiencia de lo oscuro, el cálido roce de la muerte, un instante de éxtasis para mí, heredera de todo jardín prohibido.

(*OC,* 300)

[Night, night again, the masterful knowledge of darkness, the warm brush of death, a moment of ecstasy for me, heir of every forbidden garden.]

Once again, the poet is heir to "every forbidden garden," clearly the realm of death, as the references to night, darkness, and death itself make evident. But the garden is also the province of poetry, "the place where everything is possible," Pizarnik has said elsewhere,[9] and it provides "an instant of ecstasy," the moment where death is transformed into endless poetic possibilities.

At this point we have come full circle. At the beginning of our tracing of death as a central element in Pizarnik's texts, it was associated with "nada," an absence. But now we learn that this term has become, in an apparent paradox, the essential ingredient of her poetic process. Death has become, in fact, the primary poetic element, as both "nada" and "jardin prohibido," thus proving Jurii Lotman's statement that "a word in poetry may not equal itself and may even be its own antonym."[10] The explanation for this apparent reversal from death-as-absence to death-as-creative-source in Pizarnik's poetry can be further clarified. Death is repeatedly described as the "other side," which permits the separation of the poetic voice into two selves: the present searching one and the absent one from the realm of death. The resulting tension and interplay between those two voices opens up the poetic process in these texts, a process that the first two poems in *Arbol de Diana* begin to explain more explicitly.

He dado el salto de mí al alba.
He dejado mi cuerpo junto a la luz
y he cantado la tristeza de lo que nace.

(*OC,*201)

[I have jumped from myself to the dawn.
I have left my body next to the light
and I have sung the sadness of what is being born.]

This poem recapitulates what we have already learned, a separation of self into both present self ("from myself," "my body") and absent self ("dawn": childhood or death). In spite of the references

to birth ("alba": the birth of a new day; "a la luz": a possible play
on "dar a luz," to give birth; "nace": to be born), the result here
is a sad song, since birth is the beginning of childhood, which, as
we have seen in other poems, represents the lost, dead, and absent
facet of the poet.

When we examine—on the critical level—the constant interaction between these two facets of the self, we see that the tension
between life and death determines the unique poetic voice of these
texts. A striking description of this process comes in a poem whose
title, after the foregoing discussion, is almost self-explanatory: "El
sueño de la muerte o el lugar de los cuerpos poéticos" (The dream
of death or the place of poetic bodies). Fittingly, this long prose
poem begins by placing the first-person voice of the poem within
reach of death's beck and call; the terms "canto" (song) and "voz"
(voice), which are part of the personified image of death here,
underline the inspirational role death has for the poet.

> Toda la noche escribo el llamamiento de la muerte, toda la noche
> escucho el canto de la muerte junto al río, toda la noche escucho la
> voz de la muerte que me llama.
>
> (OC, 287)

> [All night I write the call of death, all night I hear the song of death
> next to the river, all night I hear the voice of death calling me.]

From the outset, it is clear that this is to be an Orphic poem, a
temporary descent into, or—to use the term Pizarnik uses within
the poem—metamorphosis into, death; a state in which she is always aware of the contradictions with reality implied by that new
state. An oxymoronic, conflicting emotional tone characterizes the
text of the whole poem, reflecting the oppositions that determine
the text. Death is a "garden of *lilacs and ruins*"; the poet feels
herself to be "*desolately torn in her heart*" while hearing a song
of "*the purest happiness*"; she hears that song with "*a smile of
sadness*"; she speaks of her birth as "*a lugubrious face*" that nevertheless "seemed funny to me"; a *sunny* morning is described as
"lugubrious." It is this constant interplay of contradictory states
that death, the key element, orchestrates—with its "song of purest
happiness"—into an inspirational poetic source. A traditional symbol for inspiration, in fact, is wielded by a personified image of
death several times within the text, thus conveniently supporting
the semiotic evidence we have been accumulating throughout this
demonstration of death's inspirational role. Here is one example:

Y es en ese lugar donde la muerte está sentada, viste un traje muy antiguo y *pulsa un arpa* en la orilla del río lúgubre, la muerte en un vestido rojo, la bella, la funesta, la espectral, la que toda la noche *pulsó un arpa* hasta que me adormecí dentro del sueño.

(*OC*, 288)

[And it is in that place where death is sitting, it's wearing a very old dress and is *plucking a harp* on the edge of the lugubrious river, death in a red dress, beautiful, funereal, spectral, the one who *played the harp* all night until I went to sleep inside that dream.]

This image of death as a beautiful woman playing her lyre (my emphasis) is restated a third time in the next paragraph of the poem as "una bella dama que tañe un laúd" (a beautiful lady who's playing a lute).

The operative verb used here, "pulsar," links the lyre image with one of the other keys to the double-faceted aspect of Pizarnik's view of the poetic process: the mirror. Here are two examples of the mirror's being "played" as an instrument:

> Pulsaremos los espejos
> hasta que nuestros rostros canten como ídolos

(*OC*, 213)

> [We will pluck the mirrors
> until our faces sing like idols.]

> . . . pulsamos los espejos hasta que las palabras
> olvidadas suenan mágicamente

(*OC*, 216)

> [. . . We pluck the mirrors until the forgotten
> words ring magically.]

The lyrical resonance plucked from the mirrors both reflects and gives rise to the constant shifting between her two facets; she calls herself, in fact, "la niña del áspero contrapunto" (the girl with the rough counterpoint) in the poem "Densidad" (Density), where she sees the "source" (fuente) of her poetry in her own pulsating rhythms: "Yo me abría y me cerraba en un ritmo animal muy puro." (I opened and closed up in a very pure animal rhythm.)

The mirror image, as in Cocteau's *Orphée*, reemphasizes the Orphic sense of the poem about the "dream of death," which culminates in a description within the poem of a descent into the "river of death," a descent that also illuminates the Boschian imagery underlying her repeated references to death as a "garden" and even, using Bosch's own title, as a "garden of delights."

Un mundo subterráneo de criaturas de formas no acabadas, un lugar de gestación un vivero de brazos, de troncos, de caras, y las manos de los muñecos suspendidas como hojas de los fríos árboles filosos aleteaben y resonaban movidas por el viento.

(OC, 288)

[A subterranean world of creatures with unfinished shapes, a place of gestation a swarm of arms, of trunks, of faces, and the dolls' hands suspended like leaves on the cold stringy trees flapped and resonated moved by the wind.]

Significantly, it is from this surreal subterranean world (to get there she has just escaped from "the real edges of my body") that poetic reality is "born":

y mi cabeza, de súbito, parece querer salirse ahora por mi útero como si los cuerpos poéticos forcejearan por irrumpir en la realidad, nacer a ella, y hay alguien en mi garganta, alguien que se estuvo gestando en soledad, y yo, no acabada, ardiente por nacer, me abro, se me abre, va a venir, voy a venir. El cuerpo poético, el heredado, el no filtrado por el sol de la lúgubre mañana, un grito, una llamada, una llamarada, un llamamiento.

(OC, 288)

[and my head, suddenly seems to want to come out now through my uterus as if the poetic bodies were struggling to erupt into reality, to be born into it, and there's someone in my throat, someone who was gestating in solitude, and I, unfinished, burning to be born, open up, am opened up, it's going to come, I'm going to come. The poetic body, the inherited one, the one not filtered by the sun of the lugubrious morning, a scream, a call, a flame, a calling.]

Repetition has played an important role in Pizarnik's poetic language, and it continues here in the reprise of the inner pulsations that make the poetic voice within the text the source of her own poetry. Here the insistently repetitive, almost incantatory "me abro, se me abre, va a venir, voy a venir" graphically illustrates the birth pangs that accompany the forcing-out of the "poetic body" she is describing. The repetition of the syllable "ma" four times in the last sentence reinforces the birth image with its inevitable evocation of "mama" or "mamar." This whole image of the birth of a poetic sign from within the realm of death (it is also an "inherited" gift, an inheritance previously associated with the "garden" of death) is itself repeated a few lines later in the poem, in this aphoristic sequence:

> La muerte es una palabra.
> La palabra es una cosa, la muerte es una
> cosa, es un cuerpo poético que alienta en el
> lugar de mi nacimiento.

(OC, 288)

> [Death is a word.
> The word is a thing, death is a
> thing, it's a poetic body that feeds on the
> place of my birth.]

With this synthesis from her "arte poética," we are brought full circle once again—to death, the essential element of that poetics. In this poem she has summarized, and brought into clear focus in these specific lines, how death furnishes the impulse for her poetic work. This negative element clearly provides both the basis and the source for the "song" that *is* the critical poem. Death here is a "word," or "poetic body," produced by the pulsations of the counterpoint between itself and its absence: the dialogue between life and death gives birth to poetry itself. This final statement, that "death is a word," also reinforces our previous observation that the absence which death represents lies at the heart of all of Pizarnik's poems—and is their "matrix." The essential semiotic connections within these texts show that the main themes of Pizarnik's poems—death, birth, childhood, the second self—all share the "seme" (or characteristic), indeed the "archiseme," of "absence."

It is possible, of course, that this idea of absence as the basis for poetry is an original one, native to Pizarnik. But it is more likely that this and other central concerns in Pizarnik's poetry might come from other authors; Michael Riffaterre would say that there is sure to be one model that underlies her poetry.[11] In Pizarnik's case there are some exceptionally striking parallels between her poems and the theoretical writings of Maurice Blanchot, most notably his *L'espace littéraire*. To begin with, both have an overriding concern with artistic limits. Pizarnik expresses that concern with regard to poetic language, which, ideally, would be "a delirious fiesta taking place, a language without limits." But, as we have just seen, the poetic word in her texts ("the poetic body") arises out of the concern with death ("death is a word"). Why death? Blanchot raises that very question and answers it, at the same time convincingly explaining how this concept that has such a strong personal and psychological effect on all of us also can form the basis of artistic and philosophical explorations. He asks: "Why death? Because it is the limit."[12]

If art can utilize death, Blanchot says, then "art is mastery of the supreme moment, supreme mastery." According to Blanchot, this mastery of what would ordinarily be considered only a negative or absent quality provides a "contentment . . . near to Hegelian wisdom," and death now must be considered not as a negative element but rather as "absolutely positive." This concept of a negative element becoming a positive one, which both Pizarnik and Blanchot view as essential to their treatments of death, is also, in both writers, linked with "night." For both of them, this is a logical connection: "one finds death in the night," says Blanchot. But, as he explains at some length, this is the *other* night, in which an absence appears, asserting its own *presence*. This explanation by Blanchot also provides a clear textual example of how, according to Jonathan Culler, deconstruction theory would treat the "hierarchical opposition presence/absence," as occurs in the Pizarnik text. Says Culler, "We can treat 'presence' as the effect of a generalized absence."[13] The idea of absence being present also parallels the conception of death as absence *and* as creative process.

> In the night, everything has disappeared. It is the first night. There absence approaches, silence, repose, night. . . But when everything has disappeared in the night, "everything has disappeared" appears. It is the *other* night. Night is the appearance of "everything has disappeared." It is what is foreseen when dreams replace sleep, when the dead pass in the depth of night, when depth of night appears in those who have disappeared. The apparitions, the phantoms, and the dreams are an allusion to that empty night.[14]

Blanchot here helps to explain why "night" can be such an essential ingredient for the poetic process within Pizarnik's texts ("all night I make the night. All night I write"). Blanchot's "first night" contains the archiseme of absence, along with other elements sharing that characteristic: silence, rest, and, in an apparent redundance, night again. On the other hand, his "other night" is an assertion of an absence that opens up the creative perspective ("cette nuit vide"). This passage, with its apparitions, phantasms, and dreams in the "depth of the night," also helps explain Pizarnik's fascination with the dreamlike atmosphere and the phantasmagoric movement also seen in the "depths of night," particularly given the almost innate surrealist tendencies ("mi surrealismo in-

nato") to which she once admitted in an interview with Marta
Moia.[15] In "La danza inmóvil" (The immobile dance), for example,
there are "messengers in the night," and, in a following poem, there
are these unnamed entities:

> Han venido.
> Invaden la sangre . . .
> Han venido
> a incendiar la edad del sueño.
>
> (*Aventuras*, 37)

> [They have come.
> They invade my blood . . .
> They have come
> to burn up the age of dreams.]

In yet another mysterious-sounding line, we again see an assertion
of absence from within the night:

> Los ausentes soplan y la noche es densa.
>
> (264)

> [The absent ones breathe and the night is dense.]

Blanchot sums up the night-death connection, reaffirming how
this fascination with absences can be a creative resource: "But this
other night is death, which one does not find, it is the oblivion
which is forgotten, which is, at the heart of oblivion, ceaseless
memory." Pizarnik's poetry is a good example of this unceasing
memory, dwelling constantly, as it does, on her childhood. Blanchot also justifies this "fascination" with one's earliest years: "As
for childhood fascinating us, that happens because childhood is the
moment of fascination, it is fascinated itself, and that golden age
seems bathed in a splendid, because unrevealed, light."[16] Here
again Blanchot almost perfectly states the situation as found in
Pizarnik's texts: her moments of brightness are always associated
with a "golden childhood." The texts reflect her world of toys as
"a minuscule pink marionette" and as "a twinkling silver paper
doll." The importance to her poetry of the bright moments in these
nostalgic memories is underscored in the poem already referred
to, "El deseo de la palabra," where at one point she notices the
absence of some important reminiscences:

Caen niñas de papel de variados colores. ¿Hablan los colores? ¿Hablan
las imágenes de papel? Solamente hablan las doradas y de ésas no hay
ninguna por aquí.

(*OC*, 300)

[Paper dolls of different colors fall down. Do the colors talk? Do the
paper images talk? Only the golden ones talk and there aren't any of
those around here.]

That fascination with childhood, of course, becomes enmeshed
with the contradictory aspects of life/death, presence/absence,
which she sees in the child. Channeled into this poetry, that fascination becomes essential to the explanation of "absence" as the
matrix of her entire artistic production. Again, Blanchot possibly
provides a "deeply significant image" (Riffaterre's "hypogram") for
that concern: "To write is to arrange language under fascination
and, through it, in it, to remain in contact with the absolute milieu,
there where the thing becomes image again, where the image,
through allusion to a figure, becomes allusion to what is without
figure . . . in a shape drawn on (over) absence."[17] In an uncanny
way, Blanchot here, some years before Pizarnik began to write her
verse, gives what could be seen as a plausible explanation of her
poetic process. Writing is, for her, a process of fascination, but it
is an attraction presented, as she herself said, in visual and spatial
terms, since she, "at heart, united painting and poetry."[18] Like the
painter she was, Pizarnik began her development of a poem with
a view to the "negative space," the "milieu absolu" described by
Blanchot. That emptiness then determines the painting or poem.
An overwhelming absence *is there,* but it is also an "opening"
through which it allows itself to be displaced by an image, "form
sketched on absence."

As a concluding summary of that semiotic framework centered
on absence, it seems especially convenient and convincing to be
able to let three of Pizarnik's own brief texts demonstrate how
definitely stated and cohesive are the elements central to her poetry's structure. The first of these poems is essentially an outline
or list of the most basic concerns of her poetry:

sólo palabras
las de la infancia
las de la muerte
las de la noche de los cuerpos

(*OC*, 58)

> [only words
> the ones from childhood
> the ones from death
> the ones from the night of the bodies]

Childhood, death, and night together form the region of absence, of nonexistence. And that is where her poetry is born, thanks to the dialogue between her "self" and its "double," as we see in this next short poem:

> palabras reflejas que solas se dicen
> en poemas que no fluyen yo náufrago
> todo en mí se dice con su sombra
> y cada sombra con su doble
>
> (*OC*, 61)

> [reflected words that are said alone
> in poems that do not flow I a castaway
> everything in me is said with its shadow
> and each shadow with its double]

That interplay between duplicated selves takes place by means of an unsettled, reflected, and shadowy ("reflected words," "is said with its shadow") language, and against an insistent background of absence ("I a castaway"). This heightened awareness of that absence—of a personal, philosophical, and linguistic absence that surrounds the poetic voice—allows the entire poetic process to happen, a point driven home by this final, purposely repetitious text:

> el centro
> de un poema
>   es otro poema
> el centro del centro
>   es la ausencia
>
> en el centro de la ausencia
> mi sombra es el centro
> del centro del poema
>
> (*OC*, 58)

> [the center
> of a poem
>   is another poem
> the center of the center
>   is absence

in the center of absence
my shadow is the center
of the center of the poem]

This almost magically concise text, which goes to the core of Pizarnik's poetry, expresses an explicit equivalency: the center is a poem is absence is herself. The poem forms itself against an awareness of the essential absence that surrounds it, and in the process expresses the effects of that assertive absence. Instead of negating the poem, absence is the source of its creative tension. As a result, in this final poem the stark and haunting metaphysical imagery wrenched from only four repeated nouns gives these words an expressive power that comes near to reaching Alejandra Pizarnik's goal, which she shares with the other critical poets who are also looking for "a language without limits."

6
Alberto Girri: Poetry about Poetry

Long considered one of Argentina's most "difficult" poets because of his commitment to a deeply intellectual poetry, Alberto Girri (Argentina, 1919–91) was particularly concerned with the problems that revolved around language, which became an essential topic in his work. More specifically, his worries about language led him to create a magnificent demonstration of metapoetry, poetry about poetry itself, as Enrique Pezzoni has pointed out.[1] In spite of a "coldness" that has been attributed to his work over the years, mainly because of its intellectual nature, these poems about poetry actually contain a palpable tension and even a gripping sense of agony.

What Girri's texts agonize about is not just the problems with language, although that concern runs through all his poetry. These poems also have another "critical" aspect, one that gives Girri's work a particular richness within this vein of contemporary Latin American poetry: they reflect—or, more precisely, prefigure to a surprising degree—the trajectory of the most recent literary theories, beginning with the Anglo-American New Criticism of the 1940s and 1950s. Like the New Critics, Girri, at the beginning of his career as a poet, was confident in the poem as a defined object or a closed text, but he later lost that confidence and took a more searching approach. That more probing focus then made him aware of a need to look for new ways of giving validity to poetry.

Girri himself was aware of the incursions of critical theory into his work. He also admitted that other poets such as Valéry and Eliot had influenced him in this regard. Not only did those two poets incorporate their perspectives on literature into their poetry, they also had considerable influence on the literary theory of their time.[2] As we look at the ideas about literature that are ingrained in Girri's poetry, we will see that the theoretical development there prefigures and parallels, in an extraordinary way, some key conclusions made by one of the chief North American theoreticians, Murray Krieger, especially as outlined in Krieger's recent book, *Words about Words about Words.*

Krieger has been an active participant in the disputes and discussions that have contributed to the development of literary theory over the last two decades or so, so it is logical that he would be up-to-date on the state of critical theory, and that he would incorporate that knowledge into his own contributions as a theoretician. Girri, on the other hand, simply had an intuitive affinity for literary theory, and knew, or felt, or foresaw the new directions in which the theoretical discussions were heading during the sixties, seventies, and eighties. The result is a poetry in which the essential elements of poetic expression are questioned, even while the poet, through these same texts, makes his own investigations into literary philosophy. In addition, these doubly "critical" poems have, within their own texts, the theory that lies behind their genesis: the maps of the elements necessary for their own construction, reception, and subsequent reconstruction by the reader. Needless to say, this vigorous investigation into literary theory, in this case literary philosophy from within the texts themselves, makes Girri's poetry one of the most concentrated examples of critical poetry. Not only does Girri's work prefigure the development of current literary theory, it also works through the same foundational problems for poetry that have so concerned other poets such as Juarroz and Paz.

Starting with a poem from fairly early in the Argentine poet's literary and critical trajectory, we can see that it includes the essential elements of the "New Criticism." That is, this text provides a description of the poem as a static and defined object, though unconnected either to the author or to the reality it refers to. Even the title clearly explains this purpose: "A la poesía entendida como una manera de organizar la realidad. No de representarla" (Poetry understood as a way of organizing reality. Not of representing it).

> Lo que en ella place
> place a la índole de las cosas,
> inicialmente sin ir dirigidas a nadie,
> y en esencia visiones,
>   y la reflexión
> determinando que impulsos, ideas oscuras,
> cobren análogo peso, homologadas
> en sentencias que otras
> sentencias transforman,
>   apremiadas
> por lo que la poesía exige,

              lo que el poema
ha de ofrecer a la vista,
afectar a los sentidos,
              lo que tendrá
de móvil ofrenda
en un mundo estático,
y lo que el paisaje, los millones
de universales gestos piden,
                    ser formulados
en tejidos de perenne duración, claros
de diseño, voces modificando
hábitos de conceptos y categorías,
              y atendiendo
a que más allá de la verdad
está el estilo,
perfeccionador de la verdad
porque en sí lleva
la prueba de su existencia.

Escríbela,
        extrae de ese orden
tus objetos reales,
mayor miserias
que morir o la nada
es lo irreal, lo real sin objetos.[3]

[What pleases in it
pleases the nature of things
initially without being addressed to anyone,
and in essence visions,
              and the reflection
determining that impulses, obscure ideas,
gather analogous weight, homologued
in sentences that other
sentences transform,
              urged on
by what poetry demands,
              what the poem
must offer our view,
or affect our senses,
              what it will have
as a movable offering
in a static world,
and what the countryside, the millions
of universal gestures ask for,
                    to be formulated
in weavings of perennial duration, clear

in their design, voices modifying
habits of concepts and categories,
                        and making sure
that beyond truth
is style,
perfecter of truth
because it has in itself
the proof of its existence.

Write it,
        extract from that order
your real objects,
a greater misery
than dying or nothingness
is the unreal, the real without objects.]

The poem begins with a reference to the nature of things, but that nature is not the one generally associated with objects; all the references are to a mental activity—visions, reflection, impulses, ideas. These ideas are "transformed" by the demands of the poem—another personification that reflects the power the text has, especially since the text is viewed in these lines as a self-sufficient entity. As a matter of fact, it is the poem, and not the author, that will offer this vision in the form of a well-defined object, and in terms that perfectly reflect the New Criticism's ideals: "formulated in weavings of perennial duration" and made into an art that is now "beyond truth." And if the reader is not convinced, she simply has to look at the text, which is presented as carrying within itself "the proof of its existence." So far, this is an effective demonstration of the autonomous text, complete in its own terms. As such, it is also a clear demonstration of the premises of the New Criticism. Murray Krieger describes the essential aspect of that theory in this way: "[All things] were to be radically transformed by the poet . . . into a world of its own finality sealed from his personal interests as from ours."[4] Returning to the Girri poem, we thus find a double irony, beginning with the fact that the first verses quoted above are directed at the writer—which implies, of course, that this ostensibly self-sufficient text needs, at some point, to be written. And the sadness inherent in the distancing between the text and the world is described as the "greater misery." This supposed state of perfection, one must finally recognize, is artificial.

Another version of the text as a totally coherent verbal construction is found in the second section of the poem, "En la letra, ambigua selva" (In the letter, ambiguous jungle), from 1972.

La forma equivale
a convicción interna,
y la letra la emplea con vistas
a proveer al mundo de significados,
y aun para el Significado,
y aun para subyugarlo
con el prejuicio de que la palabra
traduce y vierte lo ideado.

(*P*, 93)

[Form is the same as
internal conviction,
and the letter uses it with a view
toward supplying meanings to the world,
and even for the Meaning,
and even to subjugate it
with the idea that the word
translates and pours out what was thought.]

Once again, the text constructs itself, giving the impression of impersonality, which was one of Eliot's most important doctrines. Here, made active, form uses the letter in order to "supply meanings to the world, and even for the Meaning." This pointedly demonstrates another of the New Criticism's tenets: one can articulate the meaning, or the single interpretation of each poem. It also seems to validate the idea current in that period, first pointed out by Roman Jakobson, that language has a metaphorical relationship with the world, "that a word can represent a thing."[5] Girri's text says it this way: "that the word translates and pours out what is thought."

In this earlier period of Girri's poetry there also begin to appear texts that express a growing doubt about the poem's effectiveness, especially about the language with which it is made. "En la palabra, a tientas" (In the word, gropingly) is another title that well expresses the poem's topic: the arbitrariness of language. A few lines from that poem show just how unfruitful it is:

Fallidas incursiones, intentos
de siembra que no rinden
el adecuado, proyectado fruto,
como no se recogen uvas de las espinas,
higos de los abrojos.

(*P*, 91)

> [Failed incursions, attempts
> at seeding that don't yield
> the adequate, projected fruit,
> just as you don't get grapes from thorns,
> figs from thistles.]

These "failed incursions" refer to the word or sign and to the ineffective relationship between their components, the signifier and the signified. Here the signifier does not yield the "adequate" signified that the poet "projects." The result of this failure, expressed a few lines later, is that "our usual language suffers from precariousness."

Then, several poems published in 1975 center on the dilemma that confronts the poet when he sees language—the language he has to use—placed in doubt. This situation clearly bothers the poet, even in the title of this next poem: "Preguntarse, cada tanto" (Ask yourself, once in a while).

> Qué hacer
> del viejo yo lírico, errático estímulo,
> al ir avecinándonos a la fase
> de los silencios, la de no desear
> ya doblegarnos animosamente
> ante cada impresión que hierve,
> y en fuerza de su hervir reclama
> exaltación, su canto.
>
> Cómo, para entonces
> persuadirlo a que reconozca
> nuestra apatía, convertidas
> en reminiscencias de oficios inútiles
> sus constantes más íntimas, sustitutivas
> de la acción, sentimiento, la fe;
> su desafío
> a que conjuremos nuestras nadas
> con signos sonoros que por los oídos andan
> sin dueños, como rodando, disponibles
> y expectantes,
> ignorantes
> de sus pautas de significados,
> de dónde obtenerlas:
> y su persistencia, insaciable,
> para adherírsenos, un yo
> instalado en otro yo, vigilando
> por encima de nuestro hombro
> que garabateamos;

          y su prédica
de que mediante él hagamos
florecer tanto melodía cuanto gozosa
emulación de la única escritura
nunca rehecha por nadie
                    la de Aquel
que escribió en la arena, ganada
por el viento, embrujante poesía
de lo eternamente indescifrable.

          Preguntárnoslo, toda vez
que nos encerremos en la expresión
idiota del que no atina a consolarse
de la infructuosidad de la poesía
como vehículo de seducción, corrupción,
          y cada vez
que se nos recuerde que el verdadero
hacedor de poemas execra la poesía,
que el auténtico realizador
de cualquier cosa detesta esa cosa.

                                        (*P,* 101–2)

                    [What to do
with the old lyric I, erratic stimulus,
as we go along drawing closer to the phase
of silences, the one of not wanting
to submit ourselves
to each impression that reaches the boiling point,
and because of its boiling it demands
exaltation, its song.

                    How, then, to
persuade it to recognize
our apathy, changed into
reminiscences of useless duties,
their most intimate constants, substitutes
for action, feelings, faith;
                              their challenge
that we conjure up our nothings
with noisy signs that wander through our ears
without owners, as if they are rolling, ready
and expectant,
                    ignorant
of their lack of meanings,
of where to get them:
          their persistence, insatiable,
in adhering to us, an I

installed in another I, watching
over our shoulder
what they are scribbling;

          and their preaching
that by means of it we should make
flourish both melody and joyful
emulation of the only writing
never redone by anyone
          that of That One
who wrote on the sand, won
by the wind, bewitching poetry
of the eternally undecipherable.

          We must ask ourselves this, every time
we close ourselves up in the idiotic
expression of the one who succeeds in consoling himself
about the unfruitfulness of poetry
as a vehicle of seduction, corruption,
          and each time
that we are reminded that the true
maker of poems hates poetry,
that the authentic creator
of whatever thing detests that thing.]

First, it would seem obvious that no reader of this poem could criticize its writer for a coldness in his poetry. The first question sets out the consternation that any poet who is aware of the many doubts being raised about language has to feel. Almost by definition, the poet's job requires a certain tendency toward lyric. But now, what can be done with his song? And, more important, asks this poem, what can be done with the poet (longing to be carried away by inspiration) who is inside the poet? Then comes an explanation of the situation that reminds the supposed speaker of the poem of the uselessness of his task; that futility is rooted, of course, in ineffective language. The signs here have no emitters ("they wander without owners"), and they lack signifieds. Such is the dilemma that Enrique Pezzoni explains this way: "El lenguaje de la poesía fracasa como recurso para conciliar a los opuestos: no hay éxtasis verbal que consiga salvar la distancia abierta entre la palabra y lo que la palabra nombra" (The language of poetry fails as a way of reconciling opposites: there is no verbal ecstasy that can manage to bridge the open distance between the word and what the word names.)[6]

And it is precisely a kind of mystical-religious ecstasy that the poet within the poet (an "I" installed within another "I") wishes to express: "the only writing" of the supreme being (Aquel). The poem's last section returns to the first question about what to do with the "lyric I," a return that in itself implies a certain optimism, since the previous text has explained the impossibility of attaining a lyrical poetry. But, although these final lines underline the "fruitlessness" of poetry, they also allude to the irony inherent in the poet's situation: a heightened self-awareness leads to a feeling of deception and then to a "hatred" of the process.

As an inevitable consequence of the deception through language, there has to be a new way of looking at the poem. If the New Criticism viewed the poem as a stable and defined object, more recent criticism considers the text to be fragmented and uncertain. As if anticipating the poststructuralist view, Girri, in a 1976 poem, astutely reflects this new attitude. Its title, once again, announces its perspective: "La incertidumbre como poema" (Uncertainty as a poem).

> No se conoce de poemas
> descansando instalados en el triunfo,
> la madurez, sazón pétrea.
>   Al realizarse,
> paralelamente asisten a un mudar
> de sus bríos, sutilezas,
> irónicos contrastes,
>   y a negruras, olor
> marchito de sus variaciones del ánimo,
> exuberancias, gravedades, ternuras,
> gracias, ornamentos
>   un resquebrajarse
> de la adecuación del sentido al sonido,
>   y aquellas tensiones
> por las que el efecto de conjunto se adecua
> al rotar de maneras, tonos y sellos privativos,
> y a que el arrebato de ir poniendo
> palabras en ejecución, estriba
> en recibirlas por su sabor,
>   un gusto
> como conocimiento y significación
> de lo saboreado.
>
> ¡Estén atentos,
> escribas potenciales
> soñando que el romance con cada
> poema que de sí desgranen se eternice,

prepárense más bien para verlos
invertidos, incesante inversión,
reconocerlos de tal modo
que allí donde elogiaron la vida
se leerá que la muerte es
la parte útil de la vida,
y donde ensalzaron la piedad
ésta será tenida por extravío,
y la credulidad por prudencia,
lo pésimo por bondad
lo furibundo por sano!

(*P*, 104–5)

[One doesn't know if there are poems
resting installed in triumph,
maturity, hard ripeness.
        When they are brought into being,
they also notice a change
in their energies, subleties,
ironic contrasts,
                and to blacknesses, withered
smell of their changes in spirit,
exuberances, seriousnesses, tendernesses,
thanks, ornaments,
                a cracking
in the connection of meaning to sound,
        and those tensions
through which the total effect works out
in the defeat of exclusive manners, tones, and seals,
and so that the rage of going along putting
words in use, connecting
expressions and clauses, is due
to receiving them through their flavor,
                a taste
like knowledge and meaning
of what is tasted.

Pay attention,
potential scribes
dreaming that the romance with each
poem that you pick apart will become eternal,
prepare yourselves instead for seeing them
        inverted, incessant inversion,
for recognizing them in such a way
that there where they praised life
one will read that death is
the useful part of life,

and where they praise piety
it will be taken for error,
and credulity for prudence,
tediousness for kindness,
anger for health!]

The first three lines now give the lie to the idea that the New Critics had of the poem as perfect object, which was also the same idea that Girri himself described in the first poem that we looked at in this chapter. Now, in contrast, the texts, deprived of the author's intentionality, actively "witness" the internal changes they are subject to. They are also open to a "cracking," a word similar to certain loaded terms often used in poststructural theory, such as "seams," "ruptures," and "catachreses" (Michael Riffaterre's "non-grammaticalities") of the text that allow for a deconstructive reading. The final section of this poem gives us a list of opposing elements, the "inversions" that characterize the deconstructionists' critical attitude: death for life, piety for error, anger for health, and so on. Thus, the final lines, containing only these contradictory elements (and placed within exclamation points!), emphasize the internal tension that is so important to the deconstructionists. The poem is, at the same time, a warning to the poet against artistic naïveté and idealism (the old "lyric I" of the previous poem), and a prescient criticism of the possible abuses of that deconstructive process ("the boring taken for good," for example).

In the face of this uncertainty, Girri presents another poem whose title reflects just how slippery the text is, "El poema como inestable" (The poem as unstable), but which, instead of centering around the fragmentation of the poem, addresses the poet's role. We can really say, then, that this poem is an "arte poética," even though it might seem contradictory to draw conclusions from a text whose goal is to demonstrate that the poem has no defined purpose. It may look less contradictory, however, if we also turn to the way that Murray Krieger's theories have developed. Krieger, well aware of the new poststructuralist theories, also makes an "apology for poetics," much like Girri's. This particular sharing of a theme shows clearly how well the two writers also coincide in their philosophical or theoretical development. Krieger began as a proponent of the New Criticism, but, like Girri, in spite of his predilections for certain elements of that approach, he has become thoroughly familiar with the newer poststructuralist theories and has established an original theory that combines the more

recent "scientific" approaches with the search for meaning that
was the main goal of the New Critics. Girri's apology, "El poema
como inestable," takes the same direction.

> Estado, o materia, que cuestiona
> a través del poema,
> ¿vivimos
> una vida que nos pertenece,
> o nos vive ella,
> dependientes
> de qué y cómo ella
> rasguea y tañe en nosotros?
> Y entendiendo
> que lo singular, casi nuestro
> único medio de reconocernos,
> queda en lo que trascurre
> del nacer al crecer, ser
> sanos y enfermos, morirnos,
> ¿no es vital, asimismo,
> lo ilusorio de lo fijo, movernos
> en seguimiento de lo fijo, el poema
> como vehículo, cerrado y concluso,
> para atesorar un presente
> sin detrás ni más allá,
> el poema, finjámoslo,
> acosador de lo inapresible,
> obseso registro
> de cuándo se abre la rosa,
> cuándo
> cae pulverizada una estrella,
> cuándo
>
> la hierba que pisamos
> vuelve a enderezarse?
>
> De comprender esto
> el hacedor de poemas lo es, deviene
> un hacedor de poemas,
> y en comprenderlo
> apoya su afirmarse
> por los poemas que hace,
> y la vislumbre
> de que si no fuera así sus cantos
> expresarían de él sólo lo discorde,
> y ninguna unidad, ni siquiera

mostrándolo como el gozoso, centelleante
predicado de sus cantos.

(*P,* 105–6)

              [State, or matter, that questions
through the poem,
             are we living
a life that belongs to us,
or does it live us,
       dependent
on what and how
it plucks and strums us?
             And understanding
that what is singular, almost our
only way of recognizing ourselves,
resides in what happens
between birth and death, being
healthy and sick, dying,
              isn't the illusory nature of what is set
just as important, to move ourselves
in pursuit of what is defined, the poem
as vehicle, closed and concluded,
to store up a present
with neither a behind nor a beyond,
           the poem, let's pretend,
pursuer of what is ungraspable,
an obsessive record
of when the rose opens up,
         when
a star falls pulverized,
           when

the grass that we walk on
stands straight up again?

By understanding this
the maker of poems is just that, he becomes
a maker of poems,
       and by understanding it
he supports his affirming of himself
through the poems that he makes,
          and the suspicion
that if it weren't this way his songs
would express only what is discordant in him,
and not any unity, not even
showing him as the joyful, sparkling
subject of his songs.]

The very first lines call attention to this poem's self-questioning nature ("questions through the poem"), leading the way to the central question, starting on line 15, regarding reality versus illusion. Within this long question there is a contradiction, but one that is presented as a solution to the poet's dilemma, and it is the same solution that Krieger gives in his "apology." For Krieger the text must present an "illusion of presence" that refers to its own "fictional state."[7] This is exactly what this poem suggests: what is important is what is "illusory," and the process of pretending is also necessary. We should keep in mind that, although we have seen frequent references to an unstable text, the defined aspect of the poem gets repeated emphasis here through the words "fixed," "closed," "concluded," "present," and "unity." If the poet understands "this" (esto)—the process of pretending, of giving the text what Krieger calls a "self-conscious fictionality"—then the author becomes a true "maker" *(hacedor)* of poems. This word, "hacedor," which reminds us of one of Borges's titles, implies the complexities the author has to confront. Not only must he let the "old lyric I" express itself; the author must also have "multiple consciences" of both the reading and writing processes. As a consequence, the text, for all its irony, becomes an affirmation of the entire poetic process, precisely the goal that Krieger is also after.

Existenciales, the title of Girri's 1986 book of poems, continues to reflect the need for affirmation, since it implies both the fact that the poems exist and the existential, or Sartrean, idea that the act of affirmation is the only thing that justifies existence. In spite of that insistent affirmation on several levels, there are also traces, in the more recent poems, of the futility expressed in some of the earlier poems.

POR ASOCIACIONES LIBRES

Por asociaciones libres,
eximirnos de la razón,
       desmentirla,

     dar por bueno
que puedan arrebatársele
las crías a una loba,
sin penetrar en su guarida,
      o que redondas y ovales
superficies, monedas y espigas,
sin dificultad se deslicen
en una muesca cuadrada,

mantener nuestra habla
en la opacidad,
                          de la vana
cháchara pasando a decirnos
que nada de lo que intente denotar
alcanzaría su propósito, alivio,
                ni aun los susurros
en la oreja de moribundos,
               desvirtuar opuestos
volverlos neutros,
             lo frío que deja
de luchar contra lo cálido,
          lo imponderable resistiéndose
a ser medido con lo que tiene peso;

              ¡incongruencias,
para pausa de nuestros afanes,
             y que respondan
a un solo efecto:
           aligerar, sin lastres la cabeza
en todas las quietudes,
             desde la más fútil, el lecho,
hasta el inane sosiego del polvo,
bajo el intenso, intensificado
claror celeste,
              cuando bandadas
de grullas nos rocen
dibujando en el aire letras
sin conocer la escritura,
la Escritura![8]

[THROUGH FREE ASSSOCIATIONS

Through free associations,
freeing us from reason,
                denying it,

         thinking it's all right
that they can snatch away
her young from a wolf,
without going into her den,
         or that round or oval
surfaces, coins and blades
slide into a square notch
with no difficulty,

maintaining our speech
in the opacity
                          of the vain
chatter coming by to tell us
that nothing of what it's trying to denote
would attain its purpose, relief,
                    not even the whispers
in the ears of the dying,
                    misrepresenting opposites
making them neutral,
                    cold that stops
fighting against hot,
                    the imponderable resisting
being measured with what has weight;

                    incongruencies,
for a pause in our labor,
and that respond
to a single effect:
                    lightening, the head with no ballast
in all quietudes,
                          from the most futile, the bed,
to the inane calmness of dust,
under the intense, intensified
blue clarity,
                    when bands
of cranes touch us
drawing letters in the air
without knowing the writing,
the Writing!]

The impossibility of clinging to what is rational is what the first lines emphasize, with the expressions "freeing us" and "misrepresenting it." The only affirmative statement in the text, "maintaining our speech," is undermined by the many expressions of language's ineffectiveness. "Opacity," "vain chatter," "nothing of what it tries to denote would attain its purpose," "misrepresenting," "incongruencies," "futile," "inane"; all because it is inevitable that meanings "slide away from" their signifier. The image with which the poem ends surprises us, because it is a juxtaposition that creates an enormous incongruity. It contrasts the futility of the letters—drawn by cranes almost humorously described as illiterate (not "knowing the writing")—with the nostalgic and agonized cry that could well come from the "old lyric I," yearning for "the Writing" (la Escritura), with a capital letter. It is still possible to long for the ingenuous, but beautiful, ideal of a stable language, even when language itself demonstrates its own deficiencies.

Another expression of language's instability is found in "Leer del revés" (Reading from the back side), a poem from another of Girri's later books, *Monodias* (Monodies) (1985). The poem begins with a description of the act of reading ("continuing on to the poem, / its possession / of the unforeseen in the common, / a crystalizing of the sayable"), and it ends with these lines that underline the lack of a true connection between language and reality:

> y un después,
> donde las enunciaciones del poema
> quedaron disueltas,
> circunstanciales víctimas
> de lo real volviendo
> a su inmediatez tan contigua
> que está más allá del lenguaje.[9]

> [and an afterward,
> where the enunciations of the poem
> stayed dissolved,
> circumstantial victims
> of the real returning
> to its very contiguous immediacy
> that is beyond language.]

Even in spite of these incongruities, the poems, in the pattern drawn by the other texts of *Existenciales*, continue affirming their own existence, as we see in these lines from "Dormir que hace el poema" (Sleeping that makes the poem).

> El poema,
> desprendido de la visión,
> y del que no podrías
> explicar, sólo ofrecerlo,
> y ofrecerlo
> en homenaje a lo recibido,
> pero no su enigma . . .

(*E*, 42)

> [The poem,
> detached from the vision,
> and which you could not
> explain, only offer it,
> and offer it

in homage to what is received,
but not its enigma . . .]

These lines can be seen as a summary of the "arte poética" already demonstrated. The poem no longer has any ties to the author, nor with his intentions. It is "detached" from them. Nor does it have a single explication (although I am giving *this* explanation, it is with full awareness of its possible deficiencies). In spite of all this, the insistent repetition of "ofrecerlo" (offering it) makes us see the need for the poem's creation and for making it exist, although the act of "offering" is a rather resigned or undynamic term: the poet is saying, in effect, "here it is." In addition, the text handed over in this way will never be able to provide an explanation of all the contradictions inherent in this process; its "enigma" cannot be completely demonstrated. A more positive view that follows these same ideas is found in *Tramas de conflictos* (Plots of conflicts), from 1988. The title indicates the direction these poems will take, because of their language's internal contradictions. The key poem for our purposes has as its title the word "Hacedor" (Maker), which has already played a central role in another important Girri poem. As defined by this text, the control and confidence the poet has is surprisingly impressive, given all of the uncertainties expressed in the prior poems and in the book's title.

Sin pestañear, ni relajarse,
no impaciente,
          puesta su mira
en un difuso jadeo, contenido,
y que asomará, él
lo forzará a salir,
                    y aproximársele,
no casual, inintencionado,
sino porque lo tienta,
          lo provoca
a labrar en su espacio,

          y por lo que él
como hacedor advierte:
          sólo el poema
puede ser poema,
          igual que sólo
los insectos son insectos,
sólo
al pronunciarse en poema

devienen genuinos los enunciados
desde el poema.[10]

[Without blinking, or relaxing,
not impatient,
            his sights set
on a diffuse breathlessness, contained,
and which will appear, he
will make it come out,
                        and approach it,
not casually, unintentionally,
but because it tempts him
                        it provokes him
to work in its space,

            and by what he
as a maker advises:
            only the poem
can be poem,
            just as only
insects can be insects,
only
when they are pronounced in the poem
do the declarations from the poem
become genuine.]

The maker's attitude is one of calm, as we see in the three positive expressions in the first lines. And he is conscious of his goal—
he has his sights set—in spite of the fact that it is toward a diffuse
gasping, another way of referring to the words that "wander without owners," as a previous poem put it. As a result of his effort
the poem will be able to "appear," as the three verbs in lines 5
to 7 point out. The entire process is intentional—"not casually,
unintentionally." And the reason for all this resolute activity is the
revelation that, despite its unstable language, "only the poem can
be poem" and, even more important, that the words of the poem,
with all their fluctuations, "become genuine." Again these verses,
and the other poems they represent, as texts, both elaborate and
demonstrate the same apology that the critic Murray Krieger articulates. Krieger expresses basically the same idea, but more succinctly: "I seek to maintain this power for creating poetic identity
in language despite language's normal incapacities." [11]
    It is precisely this balance between incongruities, precarious as
it always seems to be in these texts, that keeps Girri's poems
teetering toward the creation of "poetic identity." Always in the

forefront, the difficulties with language that confront the poems' "maker" are nevertheless overcome through the self-conscious and intellectual arguments that make up these texts. In short, the "old lyric I" has been put into use in order to show us just how complex the new, self-aware poem must be.

Jorge Luis Borges turns this formula around. He would rather see the complexity worked out ahead of time, so that the poet can then go on to aim for a poem of apparently absolute simplicity. The key, as we will see, is his concept of "*secret* complexity," in contrast to the overt emphasis that Girri places on the complexity that is inherent in the critical poem.

7

The "Secret Complexity" of
Jorge Luis Borges's Poetry

Ever since the final years of the Ultraist decade of the twenties in Argentina, Jorge Luis Borges (Argentina, 1899–1986) tried to undo or to discredit almost everything that he believed or wrote during those years. This purposeful rejection of what was, after all, a synthetic approach to art, a catchall of avant-garde theory and practice, led him into new areas of literary investigation that placed him once again paradoxically in the forefront of current theoretical development. In fact, Borges is now commonly mentioned in the same breath with some of the leading poststructuralist theoreticians. It is well known by now that many of those thinkers about literature, particularly the French-language ones—such as Maurice Blanchot, Michel Foucault, Gérard Genette, and Jacques Derrida—have used Borges as a starting point for certain of their concepts.[1] Their interest in Borges has generally stemmed from themes found in his prose fiction. Borges's poetry, in its own ambitious trajectory, actually expands on some of those same themes.

Although Borges rejected the militant tone of his early Ultraist pronouncements, as well as a belief in the supreme powers of the metaphor they expressed, he kept trying, in a more unassuming way, to discover—to rescue—the basis for a true poetic image. In contrast to the Ultraists' contrived metaphors—which ranged from difficult to brilliant to silly as they tried to bring together ever more "distant realities"—Borges later "modestly" advised us that his more mature poetry had a "secret complexity" underlying its apparently ordinary language.

Such "secret complexity" is the key to the critical poetry that Borges cultivated over the last twenty-five years of his life. Unfortunately, the "secret" part has its own very complex elements. Underlying that secret is Borges's skepticism toward language, which fits in with his general skepticism toward the world, as Arturo Echavarría has pointed out,[2] an attitude also shared by the other critical poets we have been discussing. Even Borges's prose writing owes its original and easily identifiable technique to his belief that language does not have the ability to "name" things, as Sylvia Molloy has shown in her article on "simulacrum and textual causality" in his fiction.[3] This concern becomes an even greater dilemma for the poet, as Borges explains in his postscript to *Historia de la noche* (1977):

> La materia de que dispone el lenguaje, es, como afirma Stevenson, absurdamente inadecuada. ¿Qué hacer con las gastadas palabras—con los Idola Fori de Francis Bacon—y con algunos artificios retóricos que están en los manuales?[4]

> [The material that language is made up of is, as Stevenson affirms, absurdly inadequate. What can be done with the worn out words—with Francis Bacon's Idola Fori—and with some rhetorical artifices that are in the manuals?]

And he then elaborates on the "inadequacy" of what he elsewhere calls "ambiguous language":

> Whitehead ha denunciado la falacia del diccionario perfecto: suponer que para cada cosa hay una palabra. Trabajamos a tientas. El universo es fluido y cambiante; el lenguaje, rígido.

> [Whitehead has denounced the fallacy of the perfect dictionary: supposing that there is a word for each thing. We grope our way along. The universe is fluid and changing; language, rigid.]

That "fluid" universe makes the idea of a "rigid" language a fallacy, as Borges often shows. Sylvia Molloy puts it this way: "Borges delights in pointing out the transformations of a word repeated and yet different, the many ways in which a term, or a series of terms, considered fixed and final, may drift."[5] This is looking very much like the troubled view of language that we saw in Paz and Juarroz and some of the French thinkers. In fact, considered as fluid and drifting, the word now almost fits Jacques Derrida's concept of the "floating signifier" (*signifiant flottant*), which results from "the absence of a transcendental signified" (*l'absence de signifié transcendentale*).[6] Derrida's term for that ungraspable sign is the "trace,"[7] which Borges again almost echoes with the words "vástago" (descendent) and "reflejo" (reflection) in these two selections from the poems "A Johannes Brahms" and "Juan 1,14":

Mi servidumbre es la palabra impura,
Vástago de un concepto y de un sonido;
Ni símbolo, ni espejo, ni gemido,
Tuyo es el río que huye y que perdura.

(488)

[My obligation is the impure word,
descendent of a concept and a sound;
neither symbol, nor mirror, nor moan,
yours is the river that flees and that remains.]

He encomendado esta escritura a un hombre cualquiera;
no será nunca lo que quiero decir,
no dejará de ser su reflejo.

(319)

[I have entrusted this writing to any man at all;
it will never be what I want to say,
it will be nothing but its reflection.]

In Borges's later poetry this inability to "name" and the frustration with a "worn-out" and "ambiguous" language are ever-present concerns; his famous poem "El otro tigre" (The other tiger) from *El otro, el mismo* (The other, the same) (1969), clearly illustrates this preoccupation, which carries into all of the subsequent volumes. In the last line of the first quotation above ("yours is the river"), we see part of the reason why the inadequacies of language hold such fascination for a writer whose favorite topic is time. For Borges, the failings of language are linked with human weaknesses, since both share a temporal nature; language is both worn out and undermined by time (a "fluid and changing universe"), as are the people who use that language. But he is not content to stay at this skeptical level; he does not simply turn the "game of signification," as Derrida would call it, into a "spiral of echoes" (in Octavio Paz's phrase). We could start our look at the other side of this coin, as it were, with the prologue to *La moneda de hierro* (The iron coin). In this essay, as he discusses the limitations of art, Borges points out that in spite of its shifting meanings, language—the word— literally has a future:

Cada sujeto, por ocasional o tenue que sea, nos impone una estética peculiar. Cada palabra, aunque esté cargada de siglos, inicia una página en blanco y compromete el porvenir. (469)

[Each subject, however occasional or tenuous it may be, imposes a peculiar aesthetic on us. Each word, even though it may be loaded down by centuries, initiates a blank page and compromises the future.]

In the face of an impure language and his own mortality, he insists on establishing a poetry with a durable meaning, and this insistence is personal and solidly affirmative, in spite of the "secret" (and ever so "critical") aspects that this process will entail.

The first way in which Borges's texts face up to an ambiguous language is by demonstrating how a word "loaded down by centuries" can have an almost unlimited richness and a multiplicity of meanings. The well-known poem "El otro tigre" does just that, showing that, as Roman Jakobson says, "the context is variable and each new context gives the word a new signification. In that fact resides the creative force of the literary sign."[8] "Blake," a poem in *La cifra* (The cipher), contains the same kind of assertion about its subject, the rose, saying it "can be" a long list of possible things.[9] It is important to note that Borges is not casual about selecting these subjects: both the rose and the tiger are words that already have poetic (or as Borges would say, "archetypal") associations, and as such they are what Greimas would term "classemes." Another poem on the same topic, with the English title "The Unending Rose," carries this idea of a multiplicity of meanings within a single word—much like Lacan's "chain of signification"—to an almost unlimited degree, a concept reinforced by the title of the book that contains it: *La rosa profunda*. That adjective, "profundo" (deep), is one that Roberto Juarroz also uses in his *Poesía vertical* in order to indicate the unlimited verticality—the open-ended depth of signification—of the poetic word. At the end of "The Unending Rose" it is evident that "the rose" has taken on a wealth of associations. Addressing the rose, the poet says:

> Cada cosa
> Es infinitas cosas. Eres música,
> Firmamentos, palacios, ríos, ángeles,
> Rosa profunda, ilimitada, íntima,
> Que el Señor mostrará a mis ojos muertos.
>
> (465)

> [Each thing
> Is infinite things. You are music,
> Firmaments, palaces, rivers, angels,
> Profound rose, unlimited, intimate,
> That the Lord will show to my dead eyes.]

An awareness that the word in poetry has the potential to evoke a vast range of meanings within the reader underlies, then, all of Borges's mature poetry, and is an important part of his poetry's "secret complexity." Although in "The Unending Rose" Borges shows how a word's endless implications can provide poetic depths, he does not focus exclusively on this idea, which some poets also see as the way to unlimited expression; for Roberto Juarroz, as we saw, the open-ended signifier is the key to a *poesía explosiva*. Rather, Borges seems to turn his back on this penetrating vision of what an ambiguous and unlimited language can do, incongruously insisting on *consciously* disregarding that knowledge. He explains the contradiction in his poem "El ingenuo" (The naïve person) from *La moneda de hierro*:

Cada aurora (nos dicen) maquina maravillas
Capaces de torcer la más terca fortuna;
Hay pisadas humanas que han medido la luna
Y el insomnio devasta los años y las millas.
En el azul acechan públicas pesadillas
Que entenebran el día. No hay en el orbe una
Cosa que no sea otra, o contraria, o ninguna.
A mí sólo me inquietan las sorpresas sencillas.
Me asombra que una llave pueda abrir una puerta,
Me asombra que mi mano sea una cosa cierta,
Me asombra que del griego la eleática saeta
Instantánea no alcance la inalcanzable meta,
Me asombra que la espada cruel pueda ser hermosa,
Y que la rosa tenga el olor de la rosa.

(486)

[Each dawn (they tell us) fabricates marvels
Capable of twisting the most stubborn fortune;
There are human steps that have measured the moon
And insomnia devastates years and miles.
Public nightmares lie in wait in the blue
And make the day gloomy. In the sphere there is
Nothing that is not another or contrary thing, or nothing.
Only the simple surprises disturb me.
It amazes me that my hand may be a certain thing.
It amazes me that the Greek's
Instantaneous Eleatic arrow does not reach the unreachable goal,
It amazes me that the cruel sword can be beautiful,
And that the rose can have the smell of a rose.]

The poem is, in spite of its title, anything but a reflection of naïveté. To be sure, it is *about* the voice in the poem thinking himself naive. And following the lead of the title, we will most likely read the poem as such: as an expression of bewilderment in the face of modern "progress" and a preference for a contemplation of the (not so simple) "simple surprises." But I think we can also read these lines as a description, or perhaps an allegory, of the new poetics that we are watching Borges develop. For this reading, "El otro, el mismo" would have been a more fitting title. Here, the poem's first half is a demonstration of "modern" or avant-garde poetics, and the second half a listing of the now preferred "simple surprises" (or secret complexities—it's pretty much the same thing, as we will see). The opening seven lines are constructed in a way that makes them representative—technically—of the kind of exotic images that have characterized all modernist poetry, and their subject matter also reflects developments of modern society. This imagery becomes almost a parody of avant-garde verse. As in the Ultraists' poetry there is dehumanization: human elements are referred to through metonymy (human steps, insomnia, public nightmares), but the images in these lines are formed by the Ultraists' favorite means, personification ("each dawn fabricates marvels," for example). The verbs used are in the Creationist mold— dynamic and assertive (fabricate, twist, measure, devastate, lie in wait). At the end of these seven verses ("there is nothing that is not another or contrary thing"), the text restates Borges's frequently expressed belief that there is an excess of analogies and nihilistic pessimism in both the world and in language.

In contrast to that conscious "modernity" of both expression and content, the second half of the poem deals with unremarkable things that nevertheless "astonish" the author, and the style changes to an apparently flat and proselike one, as the poem maintains its strict form, with its fourteen-syllable lines and consonantal rhyme. How can these simple things (the hand and the rose's smell, at least, have no obvious complexity at all) "astonish" the Borges whom we see in this poem? They cannot surprise him if he is truly naive. But there is a complexity to these things if one is aware of it, or has pondered what lies behind those simple phenomena. Why do humans have two hands and two feet, why do we have five fingers on each hand and not two or eight, for example? Why does a rose smell like a rose and not a lilac or a skunk? How can a sword that has the function of killing also be beautiful? Contrary to the title, the poet here has decided *not* to be naive, *not* to accept the apparent simplicity of these "obvious" things. This is a conscious decision made out of a deep philosophical awareness. In the light of this poem we can now more easily see what lies behind the term "secret complexity" in this statement from the prologue to *El otro, el mismo*:

> Es curiosa la suerte del escritor. Al principio es barroco, vanidosa-mente barroco, y al cabo de los años puede lograr, si son favorables los astros, no la sencillez, que no es nada, sino la modesta y secreta complejidad.[10]

> [The writer's fortune is curious. At first it is baroque, vainly baroque, and over years he can reach, if the stars are favorable, not simplicity, which is nothing, but, instead, a modest and secret complexity.]

Like the "simple surprises" of the previous poem, the "secret complexity" here is Borges's understated rebellion against the more obvious "baroque" difficulties of modernist or imagist poetry. But the answer does not lie in simplifying the text. That, Borges says, would be "nothing." Borges, typically, doesn't tell us exactly what he has in mind here. Rather, we are left to ponder a bit, and if we do that we soon realize the only things left to be simplified are the author and the reader. As contradictory as this new turn seems, after all of Borges's demonstrations of the problems inher-ent in language, we can now see the secret complexity as being the need to consciously disregard all those problems. This would be difficult, of course, and Borges has several poems that explore a more direct way around the problem of a fluid language. In "Brown-ing resuelve ser poeta" (Browning resolves to be a poet) Borges explains one possible, if merely wishful, plan of attack against ex-actly that other kind of critical poetry, including his own, which seems always to look for difficulties:

> Como los alquimistas
> que buscaron la piedra filosofal
> en el azogue fugitivo,
> haré que las comunes palabras
> —naipes marcados del tahur, moneda de la plebe—
> rindan la magia que fue suya
> cuando Thor era el numen y el estrépito,
> el trueno y la plegaria.
>
> (424)

> [Like the alchemists
> who looked for the philosophers' stone
> in fleeting mercury,
> I will make the common words
> —cards marked by the gambler, common coins—

produce the magic that was theirs
when Thor was divine and noisy,
thunder and prayer.]

This idealized approach to language that the poet plans to create
will have two important aspects. It will involve magic and alchemy
and will want to create a *hard* word ("stone," "coins") out of what
is now a fluid medium ("fleeting," "mercury"). The magic is associated with the far removed past—the time of the Vikings. Another
poem recalling this same epoch and with a similar insistence on
solid words is "Un sajón" (A Saxon).

Era tenaz. Obraron su fortuna
Remos, redes, arado, espada, escudo;
La dura mano que guerreaba pudo
Grabar con hierro una porfiada runa.

[He was tenacious. These things worked out his fate:
Oars, nets, plow, sword, shield;
The hard hand that fought was able
To carve with iron a stubborn rune.]

The second line here consists of only five words—five simple,
hard, essential, and almost symbolic things. Their importance is
even dynamic, since they are the personified subject of the verb
"obrar" (work). *They* were the *real, active* protagonists. The person, who is even reduced metonymically to a hard hand, nevertheless was able to carve out a solid and lasting image, a rune, into
stone. This poem's final four stanzas further describe the original
process of language formation, which had the magical quality
Borges is working toward in his own verse.

Para cantar memorias o alabanzas
Amonedaba laboriosos nombres;
La guerra era el encuentro de los hombres
Y también el encuentro de las lanzas.

Su mundo era de magias en los mares.
De reyes y de lobos y del hado
Que no perdona y del horror sagrado
Que hay en el corazón de los pinares.

Traía las palabras esenciales
De una lengua que el tiempo exaltaría
A música de Shakespeare: noche y día,
Agua, fuego, colores y metales.

Hambre, sed, amargura, sueño, guerra,
Muerte y los otros hábitos humanos;
En arduos montes y en abiertos llanos,
Sus hijos engendraron a Inglaterra.

(204)

[To sing of memories or praises
He coined laborious names;
War was the collision of people
And also the clash of spears.

His world was one of magic on the seas,
Of kings and wolves and fate
That does not pardon and of the sacred horror
That lies in the heart of the pine groves.

He brought the essential words
Of a language that time would raise
Into Shakespeare's music: night and day,
Water, fire, colors, and metals.

Hunger, thirst, bitterness, sleep, war,
Death and other human habits;
In arduous forests and in open plains,
His children will produce England.]

Even for the purpose of singing, the archaic linguistic development is described here as a hard, solid "coining" operation (the new, solid word could well be seen, then, as a "moneda de hierro," the title of Borges's 1976 book). But this was a magical, longed-for world, where such an immediate and unmediated relationship between the word and the world could still exist. Significantly, those iron coins are "essential words" describing "human habits," the words and the functions to which Borges wants magically to return through the "alchemy" he mentioned in the "Browning" poem. This recapturing of a magical experience with the most ordinary words recalls the astonishment seen in the four-times-repeated "me asombra" (it astonishes me) that Borges expressed in connection with "simple" things in the poem "El ingenuo"; those lines in turn are summarized in this one from "El mar" (The Sea): "the astonishment that elemental things leave."

Borges makes even more explicit his attraction to ancient linguistic origins, to a "language of the dawn," as he calls it, in "Al iniciar el estudio de la gramática anglosajona" (On beginning the study of Anglo-Saxon grammar), from the same book.

Símbolos de otros símbolos, variaciones
Del futuro inglés o alemán me parecen estas palabras
Que alguna vez fueron imágenes
Y que un hombre usó para celebrar el mar o una espada;
Mañana volverán a vivir,
Mañana *fyr* no será *fire* sino esa suerte
De dios domesticado y cambiante
Que a nadie le está dado mirar sin un antiguo asombro.

(155)

[Symbols of other symbols, variations
Of the future English or German are these words
That at one time were images
And that a man used to celebrate the sea or a sword;
Tomorrow they will live again,
Tomorrow *fyr* will not be *fire* but rather that kind
Of domesticated and changing God
Which nobody is allowed to see without an ancient astonishment.]

Again it is the original word as metaphor ("symbols of other symbols"), along with the experience of the emotional relationship between word and element, that Borges describes here. And he wants the ability to use that new/old word in order to "compromise the future" ("tomorrow they will live again"). The desired effect will be to once again experience a sense of astonishment that goes back to the original magical relationship—an "ancient astonishment."

Of course, it is not that easy. And Borges knows that. On the one hand there is the ideal of the "iron" word, coined out of an indelible experience. On the other is the continuing awareness of a failed language. In the "Inscription" at the beginning of *Los conjurados* (The conspirators), his last book of poetry, Borges writes of the tension that develops between the magic of the pure experience and the uncertainties of a fluid language:

Escribir un poema es ensayar una magia menor. El instrumento de esa magia, el lenguaje, es asaz misterioso. Nada sabemos de su origen. Sólo sabemos que se ramifica en idiomas y que cada uno de ellos consta de un indefinido y cambiante vocabulario y de una cifra indefinida de posibilidades sintácticas. Con esos inasibles elementos he formado este libro.[11]

[To write a poem is to practice a minor magic. The instrument of that magic, language, is quite mysterious. We know nothing of its origin. We only know that it branches into different languages and that each one of them has an indefinite and changing vocabulary and an indefinite cipher of syntactic possibilities. With those ungraspable elements I have formed this book.]

The beginning of a poem from *La cifra,* called "Happiness" (La dicha), brings up this very same quandary. The last line of the poem indicates at least part of its resolution, and thus the happy title. Here are its first lines:

El que abraza a una mujer es Adán. La mujer es Eva.
   Todo sucede por primera vez.
   He visto una cosa blanca en el cielo. Me dicen que es la luna, pero
   qué puedo hacer con una palabra y con una mitología.

(43)

[The one who's embracing the woman is Adam. The woman is Eve.
   It's happening for the first time.
   I've seen a white thing in the sky. They tell me it's the moon, but
   what can I do with a word and with a mythology.]

Here he asks not what he can do with just any word, but the moon, a subject scorned during the Ultraist period as being nothing but an outworn poetic cliché (just recall the Ultraists' scorn for Lugones's *Lunario sentimental*). The poem's last line, as mentioned, provides an additional, if not the essential, clue to the equation that will allow us to see further into Borges's "secret complexity":

El que lee mis palabras está inventándolas.

[The one who reads my words is inventing them.]

The reader's response, an active and creative one—an invention—is an important part of the solution. A further, final, clarification of this whole equation comes together in the poem "La luna" (The moon), which explains the "secret" of how that most outworn of words—"luna"—can be used even one more time.

El secreto, a mi ver, está en usarla
Con humildad. Es la palabra *luna*.

[The secret, in my view, is in using it
With humility. It is the word *moon*.]

That word "humility," as will shortly be clear, looks like a rather typical Borges-type understatement, except in this case it is a particularly enormous understatement. At the very least, it implies here an extreme degree of self-awareness. In the next stanza he states that he does not dare spoil the moon "with a vain image"— an indictment of both Modernismo and Ultraism—explaining in the following verses that the word "luna" already provides sufficient "complexity":

> Sé que la luna o la palabra *luna*
> Es una letra que fue creada para
> La compleja escritura de esa rara
> Cosa que somos, numerosa y una.[12]

> [I know that the moon or the word *moon*
> Is an inscription that was created for
> The complex script of that rare
> Thing that we are, numerous and one.]

Now we have the key, and it brings us, and Borges, back to the concept of "secret complexity." Here we see that it already exists in the "complex script" of human experience. On one level the complexity lies in the multiple associations a word has gathered over the centuries (and we cannot simply wish those associations away). But, at the other, the level of human complexity (which we share yet experience individually), a self-conscious ingenuousness is required. For this, the writer and, ideally, the reader, must ignore—or consciously strip away—the word's timeworn complications in order to experience a new astonishment that will match what the original fabricators of language felt when they made their first metaphorical connections between words and objects. Now a word as overused as "luna" can be experienced as an "inscription," a hard runic engraving that has all the solidity we can give it. This process is all too ironic, of course. A return to a new naïveté (an ironic concept in itself) can be attained only by virtue of a finely honed critical awareness. The "humility" with which the voice of these poems uses words is thus necessarily the result of a complex and highly self-conscious process, and those inner workings must be hidden, or secret. But they need to remain secret only for an instant—and this is yet another key. Françoise Collin provides some insightful comments on this factor of the equation. She sees in Borges's work "an intensification of the presently lived moment."[13] In his texts, she says, "the concentration of the unlimited in one instant transforms distress into jubilation."

That instantaneous "concentration of the unlimited" well expresses Borges's desire to see the problem of an unlimited, fluid word resolved through a momentary vision or "invention" of that word as a newly minted one. This is by no means a permanent or "real" solution to a fleeting language (just as Borges's famous "new refutation" of time, for all its cleverness, could not really do away with time). As Collin says, we cannot "hide the unlimited." But we can "apprehend it in a [different] mode." This different mode of perception, she continues—and this balancing of total knowledge and complete ignorance also makes Borges possibly the most "critical" of all the poets we are studying—is "a form of refutation of knowledge." Exactly. The complexity must remain secret. For Borges the key is to understand all the pitfalls that underlie language, in order to consciously adopt a new, momentary naïveté, or a willing suspension of disbelief.

Now, as sort of a postscript to this chapter, I would like to add a personal anecdote about the real Borges, who lived on Maipú Street in Buenos Aires, and how he actually responded to poetry. Two years before Borges died I was able to visit him in Buenos Aires several times. (I should mention that visiting Borges was not hard to do. To be sure, the visitor had to be in Buenos Aires, and Borges had to be there, too, and not on one of the many trips he took in his later years. One just had to call, and Borges would say when he would be free and give an invitation to come over at that time. He was gracious to everyone.) On one occasion, after we had talked for a while, I asked Borges (who was blind) if he would like me to read to him. He seemed quite pleased, and eagerly led me to his bookshelves, asking me to tell him some of the authors and titles I saw. "There is a book by Tennyson on that shelf," he said. After looking along several shelves I finally found the Tennyson, and he led me back to his couch and sat next to me, his cane between his knees. Then he asked to hold the book and leaf through the pages before I started to read. As I read he would make comments on the poems, such as, "That is a fine metaphor, isn't it?" And he would often say the last words of a line along with me. As he became more and more rapt, caught up in the poetry, he burrowed closer into my side as if he wanted to see the words through my eyes, or get into my voice. What he was trying to do, it seemed, was to get inside the words themselves. It certainly looked as if Borges, the critical poet, was able to set aside all the philosophical concerns he had about language and about problems in poetry. For those moments, at least, he seemed to have a pure, unmediated relationship with the poetic word. Most important, perhaps, his level of enjoyment could not have been higher. There was no distress, only jubilation.

8

Gonzalo Millán and "Objective Poetry"

WITH its stated goal of objectivity, the poetry of Gonzalo Millán (Chile, 1947) would seem to fall well into line with the "iron language" that Jorge Luis Borges's later poetry nostalgically longs for. In fact, Millán, in an important essay on his poetic theory, carefully emphasizes that he continues the "cosalista" strain of poetry, with its stress on material things, that stems from some of the greatest Chilean poets, especially Gabriela Mistral and Pablo Neruda.[1] That word, "cosalista," or rather its French equivalent "chosiste," is the very term that was used to characterize the flat, "dehumanized," and intensely descriptive narrative pioneered by Alain Robbe-Grillet, the foremost practitioner and theoretician of the French *nouveau roman*.

Such a "thing"-oriented literature would seem to be far removed from the philosophical and introspective texts of other "thinking poets," like Roberto Juarroz and Octavio Paz. Much of Millán's poetry does seem to avoid that intellectual bent, presenting, as it does, apparently simple visions, using clear, uncomplicated language. Even a critic as perceptive as Daniel Freidemberg sees Millán's poems this way, since they give us "very brief moments of happiness," as we "perceive the importance of the things that happen to us, especially those that can happen in very unexceptional moments, to ordinary people."[2] But we need to be aware that behind the most simple-looking poetry there often lies a deeply thought-out poetic theory. We only have to recall Borges's "simple surprises," which were not so simple; Millán's poetry has a similarly deceptive simplicity. All of Millán's poetry of "objectivity" has a self-reflective quality, to some degree, culminating in the overtly "critical" *Virus*, published in 1986.

Even though Millán's poetry prior to *Virus* is not nearly so explicitly metapoetic, all of his texts intentionally challenge the reader to respond actively in order to complete the creative process. In his first book, *Relación personal* (Personal account) (1968),[3] the reader's collaboration is made fairly easy because of the clear thematic progression of the poems. Carmen Foxley has done a thorough study of the main theme of these early poems—the process of initiation, from adolescence to a consciousness of the writer's poetic vocation.[4] Millán's groundbreaking poetry of "objectivity" appears in a more fully developed state in his second book, *La ciudad* (The city) (1979). Published in Canada some six years into the author's exile from his native Chile, this book is a product of extremely poignant circumstances and is clearly loaded with political references. It is easy—and certainly "correct," as many critics have pointed out[5]—to view *La ciudad* as a product of those circumstances and, as such, as a sociohistorical icon that, in turn, functions as a call for a heightened social consciousness on the road to a new reality.

More than a social commentary, *La ciudad* is also a challenge to the growing meaninglessness of language. On the more obvious level, of course, its skepticism toward language is a crucial part of the book's sociohistorical criticism—the poems reflect and comment on the desensitization of society in the face of a rigid military dictatorship, as well as the Orwellian devaluing of language that stems from such a tyrannical regime (Pinochet as the prototypical Big Brother of the novel *1984*). There is also, however, a clear forecast of the type of concern—which we will see most clearly in *Virus*—for a language having no fixed references. The poems of *La ciudad,* besides calling attention to problems with language, are themselves examples of a possible textual response to a language that is not just watered down, but that also floats away.

Significantly, the first poem in the collection foreshadows, at least, the language problems that surface so clearly in the more recent texts. It also exemplifies the "objetividad" that Millán has summarized this way: "From now on there will be a greater preoccupation with objects and things."[6] That is, there is an abundance of everyday objects, or things, included in the poem, presented with an equally down-to-earth language. Probably the first characteristic that the reader will notice in this and in other poems in the collection is the almost overwhelming use of repetition—Carmen Foxley goes so far as to call it "excessive reiteration."[7] Although this lead poem from *La ciudad* is a fairly long text, it is typical of the other poems in the book in its length, and needs to be reprinted here in its entirety for the reader to get the full effect of what Millán's "objetividad" entails.

Amanece.
Se abre el poema.
Las aves abren las alas.
Las aves abren el pico.
Cantan los gallos.
Se abren las flores.
Se abren los ojos.
Los oídos se abren.
La ciudad despierta.
La ciudad se levanta.
Se abren llaves.
El agua corre.
Se abren navajas tijeras.
Corren pestillos cortinas.
Se abren puertas cartas.
Se abren diarios.
La herida se abre.

Sobre las aguas se levanta niebla.
Elevados edificios se levantan.
Las grúas levantan cosas de peso.
El cabrestante levanta el ancla.

Corren automóviles por las calles.
Los autobuses abarrotados corren.
Los autobuses se detienen.
Abren las tiendas de abarrotes.
Abren los grandes almacenes.
Corren los trenes.
Corre la pluma.
Corre rápida la escritura.
Los bancos abren sus cajas de caudales.
Los clientes sacan depositan dinero.
El cieno forma depósitos.
El cieno se deposita en aguas estancadas.

Varios puentes cruzan el río.
Los trenes cruzan el puente.
El tren corre por los rieles.
El puente es de hierro.
Corre el tiempo.
Corre el viento.
Traquetean los trenes.

De las chimeneas sale humo.
Corren las aguas del río.
Corre agua sucia por las cloacas.

Las cloacas desembocan en el río.
Las gallinas cloquean.
Cloc cloc hacen las gallinas.
De la cloaca sale un huevo.

El río es hondo.
El río es ancho.
Los ríos tienen afluentes.
Los afluentes tienen cascadas.
Los afluentes desembocan en el río.
Las avenidas son anchas.
La calle desemboca en la avenida.
El río desemboca en el mar.
El mar es amplio.[8]

[Morning dawns.
The poem opens.
Birds open their wings.
Birds open their beaks.
Roosters crow.
Flowers open.
Eyes open.
Ears open.
The city wakes.
The city gets up.
Keys are opened.
Water runs.
Scissors open.
Curtains locks open.
Doors letters are opened.
Newspapers are opened.
The wound opens.

Mist rises over the water.
Tall buildings rise up.
Cranes raise heavy things.
The capstan raises anchor.

Cars race through the streets.
Crowded buses run.
The buses stop.
Grocery stores open up.
Big department stores open.
Trains run.
The pen races.
Writing runs swiftly.
Banks open their deposit boxes.

Clients withdraw deposit money.
Mud forms deposits.
Mud deposits itself in stagnant waters.

Several bridges cross the river.
The trains run on rails.
The bridge is iron.
Time runs.
Wind blows.
The trains clatter.

Smoke leaves the chimneys.
Water runs in the river.
Dirty water runs through the sewers.
The sewers run into the river.
Hens cluck.
Cluck, cluck go the hens.
An egg comes out of the sewer.

The river is deep.
The river is wide.
The rivers have tributaries.
The tributaries have falls.
The tributaries run into the river.
The avenues are wide.
The street runs into the avenue.
The river runs into the sea.
The sea is wide.]

Besides setting up the rest of the poem, as well as the book as a whole, the first section of fifteen lines suggests that this will be a text that is self-conscious about its own language. It also calls attention to the openness of the text.

Our first look at these lines needs to emphasize their function of framing the rest of the poem. With its one word, the first line determines the following verses in several ways. First, obviously, it establishes a time frame, early morning. More important, however, although it is just one word, it is a verb form. It is also dynamic—something is not just happening, it is beginning; and this action is open-ended, there is no intimation of an eventual finality here. More important yet, this word, "amanece" (dawn breaks), both determines and is developed by all of the succeeding verbs in this section. It has a semiotic connection to all of them; that is, it shares at least one seme—a meaning or activity—with each of the other verbs, particularly with the often repeated verb "abrirse" (to open up). With the morning, of course, the day "opens up," and that function is amplified throughout these lines. The second line gives a significant overdetermination to the process of becoming open. "Se abre el poema," as simple as it seems as a line, actually leads in a couple of directions. Here's what we have so far: "Morning dawns. / The poem opens." These lines give us a good metaphor—the day is seen as a poem in action. These same lines also announce that the following verses—of this poem—are going to be about the "opening" of the day. Additionally, read by itself, the second line makes a clear statement about any poetic text—that it "opens up" to a variety of readings, a multiplicity that this text, even in its apparent oversimplicity, tries to create.

This textual liberty is perhaps emphasized by the first repetition of the "opening" verb, as the birds *open up* their wings. Then they open their beaks, and the roosters *sing*. Besides referring back to the day's dawning, this verb also resonates to the idea of the poem—seen as a song—opening. The next objects to open are flowers, giving a visual focus to the text, and reinforcing the idea of the poem as image. Then the eyes and ears open up, as "the city wakes" and gets up. Besides simply representing the inhabitants of the city (through synechdoche), the eyes and ears that open up can be seen as references to the reader's (the *destinataire*'s) receptive capacity being stimulated or awakened. The city's waking and getting up, on the other hand, can be viewed metaphorically as the text's active role in its own reception or meaning, since the city, as the title has already overdetermined, *is* the poem here.

The other verb in this section, "correr," also echoes the dynamic nature of the day's breaking, and its function of opening up: curtains and locks opening, as well as letters and newspapers—reinforcing the textual aspect once again. The last of these lines, with the wound opening up, is a seemingly out-of-place reference typical of a Millán poem, at first disorienting the reader and forcing a new way of looking at the preceeding lines. After all the idyllic evocations of the opening lines comes this apparently incongruous reference to a painful wound. In addition to this perspective-shifting function, the line also gives us a good Ultraist or Cubist-style visual metaphor: the red sky at dawn seen as an open wound.

So far we have, through these fifteen short lines, a fairly succinct presentation of what Millán, in an unpublished essay, presents as "objetividad": a visually oriented poem ("la existencia óptica del poema") that presents a self-aware text ("la poesía de una conciencia en proceso"), which in turn practically demands reader involvement.

Immediately after the fifteen "opening" lines, with their emphasis on openness and repetition, comes a section of four lines, each with its reference to "lifting." This focus on "raising" something out of the openness already established in the first section gives only a momentary impression of stability. The next four longer sections all return to the insistence on openness and rapidity, through the recurring verbs "abrir" (open) and especially "correr" (run). In fact, the short, quick sentences of each line, with words sometimes jammed together, lead the reader on a breathless chase through the poem. Where does all this frantic action lead? To the water of the river and the sewer, and finally to the sea—as the last two sections focus insistently, repetitively, on terms that refer to water (water, sewers, rivers, tributaries, all of which "empty into"). So far, the poem might lead us to this reading: the daily hustle and bustle of the rat race of life seen as just part of the great river of time.

Now I would like to suggest another way of seeing the poem. Not so much an interpretation as a suggestion of *underlying* elements that work on the reader. Right away, again, we are caught up by the poem's insistent repetition. Early on, it is the sense of opening up that asserts itself, and then the constant effect of things that are running. And just what is doing the running here? Well, almost everything. But exactly in the middle of the poem we have this: "The pen races. Writing runs swiftly." Here we have specific references to writing, right in the middle of this context of words that are hurtling along, with forms of the verb "to run" coming by in almost every line. This image, or sense, of rapid language runs into the final repeated image of water running through the sewer and out to sea. At the very least, these images recall the concept of language as a fleeting and fluid medium that we have seen in poets such as Borges and Paz. And this reading of Millan's text, carried just a bit further, strongly suggests a weak or even failed language, with the image of a rapidly flowing language really going down the drain. Now, if that reading of the first poem of *La ciudad* seems to stretch away from a "poesía objetiva" in its strictest sense, then Millán's most recent book will look like a major leap.

Specifically, these more recent texts are very brief ones that do not pointedly refer to objects. Instead, they reflect on the act of writing, questioning the nature of the words that are obviously essential to that process, a turn Millán recognizes with this pointed statement in a recent interview: "Hay una crisis tremenda de no confiar más en el lenguaje" (there is a tremendous crisis of no longer having any confidence in language).[9] This is becoming a

familiar theme, here, I know. But Millán's poems are more pointed
and image-filled than anything we have seen up to this point.

This series of self-conscious texts comes from the 1987 book,
Virus, whose title is taken from a William S. Burroughs quote, "The
word is a virus." A whole cluster of brief poems at the beginning of
Virus circles around the elusive nature of the words with which
the poet is, by definition here, infected. "Jugo de bellota" stirs up
at least a faint image of what these words are:

JUGO DE BELLOTA

Bates baba. Espumas
unas exudaciones vencidas
por el uso excesivo
del verbo. Y con el zumo
glaseado de la glándula
transcribes redivivas
unas repetidas palabras.[10]

[ACORN JUICE

You whip up drool. You exude
some defeated froth
through excessive use of
the verb. And with the glazed
juice from the tear duct
you transcribe some revived
and repeated words.]

The first two verbs, which describe "the excessive use of the
word" ("batir," "espumas"), both refer to the action of whipping
up a froth, full of air and little substance. The effects of this verbal
activity are completely without substance as well—spittle, worn-
out discharges ("exudaciones"). The glazed juice from the tear
duct ("la glándula," which also refers to a secondary meaning of
"bellota" in the title, "glans penis," which would give an earthier
but similar reading) is used to form words—but what kind? Emphasis, in the title, on the surface gloss of the creative juice already
emphasizes a lack of substance in this image of word formation.
Moreover, as the text makes clear, these words are not created
directly, but are rather *re*written (transcribed), *re*vived and *re*-
peated. As in many of the poems that center around language—
especially those of other Latin American poets that we have been
looking at—this one clearly echoes the idea of Jacques Derrida

that words are always in flux, being written over and always in new contexts. Even the word "glaseado" recalls the title of one of Derrida's books: *Glas*. This echo of Derrida continues in several other short poems in *Virus*. In the next poem from that collection, for example, the whole concept of words being without substance is reaffirmed many times by the series of images that follows from its title, "Ephemeral colonization":

COLONIZACIÓN EFÍMERA

Trabando las burbujas
de aire que haces
con pequeña saliva
y una pluma fuente
hasta hoy has conseguido
esponjas, y a lo más
espumas en papel secante.

(*Virus*, 14)

[EPHEMERAL COLONIZATION

Joining together the air
bubbles that you make
with a little saliva
and a fountain pen
until today you have gotten
sponges, and at most
foam on blotting paper.]

Here, words again result in more froth: bubbles, sponges, and foam. All of these are creations full of air, obviously impermanent, as the title underlines, but especially so when they end up on blotting paper ("papel secante").

Having such precarious material to work with makes it a heavy task for the poet to write, as the images of the following poem illustrate:

HOJAS DE PLOMO

Vuelves las páginas
grises y pesadas
como el plomo
de tanto estar
en blanco, esperando
en la penumbra dorada.

(*Virus*, 15)

[LEAVES OF LEAD

You turn the gray
and heavy pages
like lead
from being white
so long, waiting for
the golden shadows.]

Heaviness is the theme of the title as well as the first lines, as the paper is described as lead, with the grayness and weight associated with that metal. The final image lends a glimmer of possible illumination, however, as the now white paper waits, as does the poet (the verb "esperando" could apply to either or both), in the golden shadows—indicating an oasis of romantic hope for inspiration and the possibility of creation, in spite of the murky nature of words and writing.

We have seen images in these first poems, but in the next one the image is basically one large, clear, visual, and plastic illustration of the process of writing that the previous poems have been describing.

PRACTICANTE

Te ejercitas con el bolígrafo
de punta retráctil
como con la hipodérmica
el aprendiz de practicante:
inyectando glóbulos de aire
y extrayendo jugo
de la porosa palabra *naranja*.

(*Virus*, 14)

[PRACTITIONER

You practice with the ballpoint pen
with a retractable tip
like the doctor's apprentice
with a hypodermic needle:
injecting air bubbles
and extracting juice
from the porous word *orange*.]

The writer's ballpoint pen is compared to a syringe—its retractable point perhaps implying the difficulty of maintaining a creative streak. But it is not pictured here as a dependable source of writing. Rather, it injects and draws out, from an empty source (a bubble of air), the substance ("juice") from the very *word* "orange." And even that word ("naranja") which provides the extracted material is lacking in substance: it is "porous." All of the difficulties of writing are here—since there is no tangible source, the writer must look to fleeting thoughts (air bubbles) and must use words that are only traces of other, vulnerable (porous) words.

Just how slippery and ephemeral these traces are becomes evident in another allegorical image formed by the poem "Sin hueso":

SIN HUESO

Alentado tan sólo
por la nube cálida
de su propio aliento,
los ojos ardientes
únicamente visibles,
el perro verbal
del esquimal escarba
y escarba
en la página de nieve,
pero nunca
entierra el hueso.

(Virus, 54)

[WITHOUT A BONE

Encouraged only
by the warm cloud
of his own breath,
only his burning eyes
visible,
the Eskimo's verbal
dog scratches
and scratches
on the page of snow,
but never
buries the bone.]

The title could just as well have been "sin huellas," since the poem shows how unstable and unfixed verbal signs are. Through its explicit key to the allegory, the "verbal" dog, the text clearly refers to the poet's difficulties with setting down words and with establishing any kind of set meaning for them. First of all, the only basis or source that the writer (the "verbal dog") has is his own inner spirit, itself a momentary thing ("the warm cloud of his own breath"). The bone (the word, or sign) that the poet wants to set into the page cannot offset the resistance that already exists toward that attempt. That resistance is here attributed to the page itself. In the image drawn by this text, the snow is the page; significantly, snow (or the blank page) can be frozen hard, as it is here, to resist any intrusions, or it can be either blown or melted away—erasing any marks that may have managed to be etched into it.

If it is indeed so difficult to write, knowing all these pitfalls and unrelenting uncertainties, then how does a poet avoid becoming paralyzed by such a daunting process? Here, in a few lines, is a partial answer:

GAZAPOS DE MARFIL

En escaso espacio
en blanco se aparean
concentrados versos
sin *horror vacui,*
creciendo duramente
como dientes
montados
los unos sobre otros.

(*Virus,* 17)

[DEVIATIONS IN IVORY

In a tiny blank
space concentrated
verses pair up
with no *horror vacui,*
growing hard
like teeth
set
one on top of the other.]

Here the title summarizes all the uncertainties associated with the writing process, but the poem's text does hint at a resolution. "Gazapos" is a word with many possible meanings, all of them related to misunderstandings with language. It can refer to sly people, to verbal lapses, to mispronunciations, to blunders, and to printing errors or misprints. Probably the latter meaning would work best as a reading of this particular title, but all of the other possibilities help establish a rich context for the poem. In fact, the title alone illustrates just what happens when a reader's mind slips from one possible meaning to another, thus allowing the sense of the text to shift and grow as well (just as it should while reading any good poem). In any case, the title certainly calls up all of the difficulties that confront a word producer. So what, if anything, happens next? This text gives a picture of one response. The key is the line, "with no *horror vacui,*" indicating that even in the face of all the known problems, and even the impossibilities of setting down a fixed text, the process must continue—and fearlessly. In order to counteract the shifts in meaning, the always changing center of every word and text, words must be set down—surrounding and covering each other ("pair up," "concentrated," "set one on top of the other"). The basic implication in this stark text is a response to the Derridean idea of the sign as mere trace. Contexts have to be formed for each word in these new texts; each new text forming a new context, which will in turn replace the one that has already shifted or blown away. The poem certainly becomes, in this reading, what Millán calls "la imagen-poema que consigue la identidad con lo representado" (the image-poem that attains identity with what is represented).[11]

It seems quite clear now that the poet is putting his "objectivity" in the service of the critical poem. In the final text the object—a taxi—is used as an allegory for the unstable sign, which has by now been pointed out so often, and for the reader's important role in overcoming the dilemma that results from that instability.

PARADERO DE TAXIS

Estos vehículos de letras
se ponen en movimiento
al leerse, sucesivamente
como los taxis detenidos
empujados por sus choferes.

Sin encender los motores
para ahorrarse la gasolina,
van ocupando el sitio libre
de los que fueron empleados.

Y después de la carrera,
estos vehículos de letras
vuelven y allí mismo esperan
otros o a los mismos lectores.

(*Virus* 18)

[TAXI STAND

These vehicles of letters
put themselves in movement
when they're read, successively
like stalled taxis
pushed by their drivers.

Without starting their motors
to save gas,
they start occupying the free space
left by those who were taken.

And after the trip,
these vehicles of letters
come back and wait right there
for other readers or the same ones.]

Here the taxis, like words—which, as "vehicles of letters," they so clearly represent—are set in motion when occupied and return to a new and static context when their most recent activity is over. Instead of trying to force some kind of lasting, unchangeable verbal meaning, the poet here opts instead for a graphically noticeable effect on the reader, who can be transported, as it were, through the power of the image, which feeds in turn on the complicity established between text and reader. That complicity, as seen in these poems, is still a rather complex process, as it was for Borges, but it's no longer so "secret."

The irony, however, is still there. These brief texts from *Virus* present brilliantly analogical verbal and mental pictures, which showcase the problems that make the contemporary text theoretically impossible. The biggest irony, however, is that these poems are facing up to that implied dilemma as they graphically expose the poems' own fallibility.

9

David Huerta: *Incurable*

IN large part, the primary focus of the critical poetry we have discussed in the previous chapters has been on the negative aspects of this new poetics. In those poems, language has been taken apart, revealed as nothing but a faint shadow, and cited as the cause of much writerly frustration. Because of that frustration with language, we have seen a great range of self-doubt in the critical poets, ranging from a near paralysis to a frantic desire to escape into a state of self-delusion. Now we come to the newest and youngest poet, who does not escape any of those problems. In fact, they seem to have landed on him intact and in totality. But David Huerta's *Incurable* (1987) is more than just a review of the critical examinations that the other poets have been revealing through their poetic texts. This recent book self-consciously (and self-consciousness is also one of the central characteristics of the critical poem) works through the problems that it finds in the various elements that go into the making of poetry. Finally, this text works, struggles hard, as it searches for a way to create art—as the title strongly indicates. Even while realizing that this art will retain the ability to undo itself, the voice within this text shows that he is an "incurable" poet. He has to keep writing at all costs, in spite of that apparently unresolvable dilemma.

He is also incurably infected by the poetry "virus," to return to Millán's title. He has been bitten by the bug that has led his predecessors into the world of verse. As a result, this book is a tour de force that not only reveals, but also revels in, the perpetual intertextuality that poetry is. This work, by including many self-aware references to literary tradition, establishes poetry as a field of constant textual interaction. These references often take the form of pastiches, both sarcastic and respectful, of some of his best-known precursors. In addition to this literary interweaving, *Incurable* incorporates and examines, with an even greater virtuosity than we saw in Alberto Girri, the literary and philosophical theories of the most influential postmodern thinkers. The inclusion of these poststructuralist ideas—chiefly those of Lacan and Derrida—underscores preoccupations with poetic language, the limits of the poem, and the resulting inability on the part of the reader to enclose the text within one single interpretation.

Clearly, a prodigious artistic maturity shows through the entire length of this long text, published by David Huerta when he was only thirty-eight years old. The son of an important Mexican poet, Efraín Huerta, David Huerta (born in 1949) began to publish books of poetry at the age of twenty-five, books that showed a fine literary education, a sharp intelligence, and a true poetic vocation, and that gave evidence, to be sure, of a poetic self-awareness. And we can find seeds of some of the concerns that become prominent in *Incurable* in these very first books. In the earliest, *El jardín de la luz* (Garden of light) (1972),[1] we see the visual orientation that characterizes all of his earliest poetry.[2] In fact, according to the poet himself, the visual focus predominates in all of his work up to the present.[3] There are also, in the early poetry, two related visual elements: the idea of light as a source of poetry and pointed references to mirrors, a Borgesian theme that appears frequently. Also relating to the visual elements in this early book is a fascination with images—especially the idea of images as a theme for poetry.

Huerta's preoccupation with language shows very clearly in *Cuaderno de noviembre* (November notebook) (1976). Specifically, this text points out difficulties in the use of language: "La palabra . . . hace su travesía laboriosa" (the word . . . makes its laborious way).[4] Even more uncertainties come when a name—a highly specific word—is used.

Es que el nombre tiene coordenadas inciertas . . . no se dice el nombre sin riesgo de sordera . . .

(46)

[The fact is, the name has uncertain coordinates . . . one does not say the name without risking deafness . . .]

Hay en el nombre fallas, esguinces y precipitaciones,
no es él una dádiva o un calor de la designación, porque su azar determina un despojo,
el existir que lo rodea sobreviven errores que aún oscurecen la "fidelidad", son un desvío.

(47)

[In the name there are defects, twists, and precipitations,
it is not a gift or a heat coming from designation, because its fortune
determines a divestment,
the existence that surrounds it, errors survive that even obscure the
  "fidelity," they are a detour.]

An indication of a possible way out of this difficulty can be seen
in the final poem of the collection, in these following lines brimming
with confidence. Images are the key here, especially the ones that
originate with the body. In addition, in these lines, breathing,
blood, and the "secret network" serve as bases for several important images that ultimately relate to language:

> Cuando respiro me adueño del mundo:
> no hay extravío, hay imágenes, la sangre está escrita en la
> secreta red del cuerpo.

(105)

> [When I breathe I become owner of the world:
> there is nothing misleading, there are images, blood is written in
> the body's secret network.]

This lack of confidence in language, along with viewing the image
as a possible solution, is also seen in Huerta's next book, *Versión*
(1978). The difficulty in representing the real is made clear in these
verses from "Index":

Cada tema entra alguna vez en el claroscuro de la palabra que lo con-
voca, la cosa, la mera cosa rala y directa, cede a la ola del lenguaje.[5]

[Each theme at some time enters into the light and dark of the word
that invokes it, the thing, the threadbare and direct thing itself, gives
in to the wave of language.]

Although the word is described here as something undefined
("claroscuro"), it is still, as these lines show, superior to "the thing"
that has to "give in" to language. Once again in this book, the
image rescues the residue of the words that do not leave anything concrete.

¿Sientes que en la imagen de esas palabras hay un trazo de ti, un río
de huellas donde leo tu gasto bordeado por la decoración de escribir,
de hablar?

(40)

[Can you tell that in the image of those words there is a dash of you, a river of traces where I read your consumption bordered by a decoration of writing, of speaking?]

There remain only "a dash," "traces," and a "consumption," very uncertain elements, and the writing in which this description is found is classified as a "decoration," another unsubstantial or unnecessary characteristic.

Along with the themes already mentioned, there are scattered references in these early books to "desire" and to an undescribed and unexplained "other" (otro). These terms would not bother us much if it were not for their centrality in the long poem, *Incurable*. And *Incurable* is long. It is a book of almost four hundred pages, full of energy and thought, which has surprised both readers and reviewers by its vitality and its size, especially since this vast work comes from a poet who has shown such doubts about the efficacy of both language and poetry. The book is a constant struggle with doubt, fear, and uncertainty, but it goes beyond merely attempting to address or resolve the problems that pursue poetry. Rather, this book's intent is to embrace poetry, to make itself a representation of what modern poetry is, within the context of *all* poetry. Finally, and perhaps most important, this long poem comprises a search for a way to transcend the very limitations that it makes so evident.

It is not easy to select only a few lines to quote in this chapter, since the entire long poem is full of essential points, but we will begin with this key section from the third page of the book:

Materia del yo, un descenso órfico en el deseo,
un tocamiento de lo que se derrama, sin centro ni asidero,
un pozo limitado por el norte de las palabras y el sur
        infernal o egipcio
de lo reprimido, postergado, diferido, abandonados en
los jardines horrendos del pasado.[6]

[Material of the I, an Orphic descent into desire,
a touch of what is poured out, without center or handle,
a bit limited by the words' North and the infernal
        or Egyptian South
of what is repressed, postponed, deferred, abandoned in
the horrendous gardens of the past.]

Huerta himself has said that *Incurable,* especially the first half, has a touch of "telquelism," and these lines do demonstrate a large debt to the newer French literary criticism, in this case to the two

Jacques: Lacan and Derrida. Throughout the whole poem there is
an "I" who speaks, and in the first line of this quote, with the
reference to the "material," or the substance, of this "I" and in its
connection with "desire," we have obvious references to the work
of Lacan. The subject who speaks, along with its various components, is one of the themes that appear with most frequency in
Lacan and in the other critics who follow Freud. It will become
obvious, as we continue commenting on the poem, that this "I"
represents more than the implicit writer—what Juan Luis Martínez
represented as the (author) between parentheses—in the text.
Once again, Huerta himself agrees, saying that "the one who
speaks in *Incurable* says 'I' but that 'I' is many; they are, we are
legion, even what is unidentifiable."[7] But here, in the second line
this "I" is linked with characteristics of maximum instability:
"without center or handle." This is pure Derrida ("puisque le cen-
tre ne lui appartient pas" [since the center does not belong to
him]),[8] and the Derridean element increases in the following lines,
where language becomes infected by this uncertainty, again with
terms taken from the French philosopher. In these lines there is
also a game with limits going on. If the well that is the descent
into desire has "the words' North," that sounds quite positive to
us: we will be able to orient ourselves by referring to the words.
But if the other pole, the South, is only made up of what is absolutely uncertain—an infernal region "of the repressed, postponed,
deferred, abandoned"—this removes any fixed or stable quality
from the North; because if one pole shifts, the other will, by definition, be equally unstable. That is to say, words also suffer from
postponement or being deferred, other characteristics that seem
to come straight from Derrida: "primarily, *différance* remits to
movement (active *and* passive) which consists of deferring, delay,
delegation, postponing, remitting, detour, slowing, putting in reserve."[9] The only thing in these lines that is not related to "telquelism" is the reference to the "Orphic" descent, one of many
surrealist elements that also reccur throughout the text.

But let's go back to the "desire" that appears in this first quote,
within the context of what is uncertain. Uncertain is exactly what
desire is, both in the work of Lacan and in that of Huerta—but
this does not mean that it is without importance. To the contrary,
farther along in the poem, the subject who speaks realizes how
desire weighs on him: "En verdad estoy sucio; cargado como una
máquina por la retícula de un *hacia,* el del Deseo" (really I'm dirty;
loaded down like a machine by the reticle of a *towards,* that of
Desire) (54). The importance of desire is underlined by the capital

letter; but what is this Desire? Here the poem says it is a "towards," implying that Desire is not anything, just a future possibility. This coincides exactly with Lacan, who sees desire as
something "unnamable." He also sees it as a lack, as something
that is not present.[10] In Huerta's text we also see precisely this
characteristic:

Y entonces comprendí que tu pecho era mi pecho y que tu
mano y su tacto
no eran sino el deseo enterrado en cada una de las palabras no dichas.

(133)

[And then I understood that your chest was my chest and that your
hand and its touch
were nothing more than desire buried in each one of the unsaid words.]

The lack here is associated with the words to be said ("no dichas"), again giving the idea a certain unnamable futurity, and also
relating to the uncertainty that the words themselves carry with
them, in the context of the poem.
No less important in this quotation is the origin of the desire—
it comes from "your hand and your touch," and this is after the
subject confuses his own chest with "your chest." Who is this "tú,"
this "you," then? An important question indeed, since the subject
who speaks repeatedly dialogues with a "you," inextricably linked
with the "I" who speaks, and this is a direct, although unstable,
relationship.

Hablo en ti, directamente, por mis intersticios.

(23)

[I speak in you, directly, through my interstices.]

It is not "I speak to you," but rather something that happens in,
or perhaps inside of, the other. Even so, it happens "directly." Not
with the voice or the mind, but rather within a part of him that is
not specific and that is impossible to localize: the "interstices" (one
of Roland Barthes's favorite words). But this relationship gets
clearer:

Hablo en ti como un espejo nómada. Soy en ti la sola palabra
        que me designa como imagen,
una fuerza escondida en tu aliento, una virtualidad que te
        recorta en lo que en mí te prepara como imagen:
eres en mí lo que habla . . .

(24)

[I speak in you like a nomad mirror. I am in you the only
    word that designates me as an image,
a hidden force in your breath, a virtuality that
    cuts you out into what, inside me, prepares you as an
image: you are what speaks in me . . .]

He keeps speaking "in you," but now as a mirror, a recurring image
in the poem (the first line of the poem is "El mundo es una mancha
en el espejo" [The world is a stain on the mirror]). This "you" now
is *seen* as a reflection of the subject that speaks, or of an aspect
of that subject. The mirror, described as nomadic, is yet another
reminder of the instability that has been associated with language.
This lack of stability is reinforced by the visual image of the complex subject, with constant reflections of the you and the I. This
you represents a "force," defined as "a virtuality," once again recalling Derrida's concept of what is postponed or deferred. But in
the end, the you (tú) is what speaks in the subject (Lacan: "in
language our message comes to us from the Other").[11] This internal
dialogue is crucial, since in large part it is what makes this poetic
text possible and its images successful, as we confirm on the next
page of the poem.

        Mis imágenes te observan con una fruición desmesurada.

                                              (25)

        [My images observe you with an unmeasured fruition.]

    The personification of the word "images" and the fact that they
"observe" doubly underline the importance of the image and of
the visual aspect in this poetry. The relationship between the you
and the I is total; the you is confused with the I. "Y quién-soy-
eres" (And who—I am—you are), says one line, and in another
part of the text we see that these two aspects coexist.

        Coexisto en ti con tus imágenes,
el reino de mí sigue tu paso.
                Seguir así, así, oyendo el
irresistible mundo que me otorgas.
. . . .
¿Cómo llegar hasta los surtidores del simulacro?
. . . .
Estas son mis palabras para ti, después de tanto tiempo,
de nuevo cargadas con el sediento perfume de las imágenes
que desearía congregar.

                                              (46)

[I coexist in you with your images,
the realm of myself follows your lead.
              To go on like this, like this, hearing the
irresistible world that you grant me.
.   .   .   .
How can I get to the supplier of the simulacrum?
.   .   .   .
These are my words for you, after so much time,
again loaded with the thirsty perfume of images
that I would like to bring together.]

It could not be clearer; the you and the I exist together. The attraction of the you is the irresistible world of its images, which take the speaker to the "providers of the simulacrum"—the poetic effect. And this effect can only be attained, once again, by means of "the images that I would like to bring together." All of this is consistent, within the context of this poem, but the "I" has to add that it also coexists with its contradictions, thus creating a tension that in effect summarizes the irony implicit in any postmodern writing, where the text exists despite its own internal contradictions.

If this tension were not obvious, the text makes even more clarifications with regard to the "you," placing it within the Freudian realm of the unconscious, in contrast with the traditional concept of language:

Huía del lenguaje en cada una de tus palabras y
lo que yo escuchaba con una respirada incertidumbre
y un sentimiento de ancho mundo,
era el rumor del inconsciente, mezclándose como un
deslizarse de fieras brillantes
por los pasadizos de mis oídos. Tu inconsciente tocó mis
oídos,
escuché el lenguaje derramándose, turbio y feraz,
por los canales sordos del inconsciente que me mostrabas.

(156)

[I was fleeing from language in each one of your words and
what I was hearing with a breathed uncertainty
and a wide-world feeling
was the murmur of the unconscious, mixing itself like a
sliding of shining wild things
through the hallways of my ears. Your unconscious touched my
ears,

I heard language pouring itself out, fertile and turbulent,
through the mute canals of the unconscious that you were showing
    me.]

Lacan, after Freud, says that "the unconscious is a discourse,"[12] and that is the situation in these lines, as it is in almost the whole poem. An unconscious language is pouring itself out. Now it seems that we see perfectly clearly who the you in the poem represents: a certain aspect of the speaker in the poem. It is not this simple, however. There are also multiples of the you and the I.

El tú o ustedes representado, múltiple y sólido, su molécula
    triturada, la zona
de su confuso manifestarse . . .

                                                      (78)

[The you or all of you represented, multiple and solid,
    your crushed molecule, the zone
of your confused appearing . . .]

It is not only a you (tú), but rather an "all of you" (ustedes), whose identity is confused and bedraggled. This, of course, is nothing but the reflection of the various aspects of the subject himself. The "I" of this poem is decentered and multiple; it even asks: "Quién es nosotros?" (Who is we?) (225), sounding like the confused narrator of Cortázar's "Las babas del diablo" (Blowup). The speaking subject even shows its feminine side:

Por el revés, hablo con otra voz; y me despierto.
Es la mujer que me sostiene sobre gasas heladas, los fríos
roces del insomnio.
La mujer que yo soy, la mujer que es yo; su rostro
limpio y fresco, de pómulos definitivos, de labios más eternos
que las piedras del desconsuelo.

                                                     (292)

[On the reverse side, I speak with another voice; and I wake up.
It's the woman who supports me on frozen gauze, the cold
brushes of insomnia.
The woman who I am, the woman who is I; her clean
and cool face, with high cheekbones, with lips more eternal
than the stones of sadness.]

There are two possibilities for this revelation. The first has its key in the word "reverse." In Alejandra Pizarnik's poetry, for example, there is a constant play of opposites: presence/absence, this side/ the other side, and so on, demonstrating the idea that in order to have presence there must exist absence. For the philosopher Derrida, this tension between presence and absence is part of the "game" that writing is. "Besides, the supplementarity that *is not anything*, neither a presence nor an absence, is neither a substance nor an essence of man. It is precisely the game of presence and absence, the opening of this game that no metaphysical or ontological concept can understand."[13] In this case it would be possible to say that the masculine needs the existence of the feminine for its own existence. Or, also, as Robert Bly frequently suggests, it is possible that the subject simply is recognizing his "feminine side."

The same thing happens, to an even greater extent, with the "tú"—the unconscious, the other. On various occasions, it is a woman, a lover, as can be seen in this passage that serves as a summary:

> Tú me abrazarás con una dulce furia, me darás el esplendor de
> la noche con tus manos fuertes de mujer adorada.
> Algo se repite, nuestro amor.
>
> (380)

> [You will hug me with a sweet fury, you will give me the splendor of
> the night with your strong hands of an adored woman.
> Something is being repeated, our love.]

In other sections of *Incurable,* the "you" is poetry itself (383), it is love in general (293, 388), and it is the figure of the "professor" (159–61). On several occasions, as we have also seen, the "you" functions as the inspirational figure, the poet's muse. The text directly alludes to this function several times, as in this image of a traditional poetic symbol: "llegarás con un cisne en los labios" (you will arrive with a swan on your lips) (190).

This internal confusion also points to the central drama of *Incurable:* the search for poetic inspiration in the face of all the theoretical, psychocritical baggage of today's literary world. Huerta's poem has that whole investigation of the unconscious, done along Lacanian lines, that we have been discussing, but it is done clearly, and finally, in the service of poetry. The desire that gives rise to the dialogues is a source of energy that drives this text. The dialogues between the "I" and the ever-changing "you" build upon that energy, generating a *need* to write. This process is thus a source of inspiration, of breathing life into what otherwise could be, for a critical poet, a futile investment. Besides this self-aware investigation into the inspirational process, the poem clearly tries to embody poetry, to surround it. *Incurable* is a puzzle, a game of intertexts, an interweaving of quotes, parodies, and emblems.

It would be impossible, even for an *archi-lecteur,* to make a complete catalog of all the intertexts and literary references in *Incurable*. At least it would be a longer and more profound study than this one can possibly be. But it is worthwhile to point out some passages that have to do with the self-referential poetic world that this text is attempting to construct. The poet shows that he is not only able to refer to the great poets of the past, but can also make his own variations on their themes. Thus he partially destroys the limits that those revered texts supposedly have, which in turn contributes to *Incurable*'s efforts to go beyond the limits associated with more traditional poetry. References to the larger poetic context into which this particular text, *Incurable,* fits are clearly part of the self-awareness that characterizes a "critical poem." Also, this process of literary references makes essential the reader's participation in the discoveries of the constant game between the poet and his artistic ancestors, a game that reveals the poet's scorn for the "anxiety of influence" that each poet is bound to feel about his predecessors.

Perhaps the most important intertext in *Incurable* is the imitation of Manuel Gutiérrez Nájera's "Mis enlutadas" (My women in mourning); here are a few lines from that poem:

> Descienden taciturnas las tristezas
>   al fondo de mi alma,
> y entumecidas, haraposas brujas,
>   con uñas negras
>   mi vida escarban.
>
> . . . .
> Y urgando mudas, como hambrientas lobas,
>   las encuentran, las sacan, [mis culpas, mis faltas]
> y volviendo a mi lecho mortuorio
>   me las enseñan
>   y dicen: habla.[14]
>
> [The taciturn sadnesses descend
>   into the depths of my soul,
> and numb, ragged witches,
>   with black fingernails
>   scratch my life.
>
> . . . .
> And silent, agitating, like hungry wolves,
>   they find them, they take them out, (my guilt)

> and returning to my deathbed
> they show them to me
> and say: speak.]

And here is Huerta:

> Pero ahora te veo, despeinado, colérico marasmo, ciega lumbre,
>   piso enlodado... Bailas aquí, bailabas,
>   visible sopa, llegando hasta mis cosas y mi extraño pensar:
>   venenoso desvío, cuchara enrojecida, brasa doliente y
>   seductora, paño de las inhumanas curaciones.
>   Hablas con esa voz, con esa voz, bailando.
>
> (81)

> [But now I see you, uncombed, furious apathy, blind light,
>   muddy room . . . You dance here, you were dancing,
>   visible soup, coming to my things and my strange thinking:
>   poisonous detour, reddened spoon, hurting and seductive
>   coal, cloth of inhuman cures.
>   You speak with that voice, that voice, dancing.]

To a certain extent, Huerta's whole poem has as its theme a variation of this premodernist poem, in which the subject who speaks insists that his witches, his sadnesses, speak to him or make him speak—a process that ties in with the use of the unconscious as source of inspiration in *Incurable*. There are other pastiches from the *modernista* period (which was anticipated by Gutiérrez Nájera), like this one that refers both to Rubén Darío and to Marcel Proust:

> —Todo es *tan* absurdo, ay—dice afectada, afectuosamente la
>   Marquesa...
> sin salón de Guermantes, sin borla ni abanico sobre la
> serenidad perfumada y horizontal del té, como
> constelaciones.
>
> (174–75)

> ["Everything is *so* absurd, ah," the Marquesa says affectedly, affectionately . . .
> without a Guermantes salon, without a tassel or a fan on the
> perfumed and horizontal serenity of the tea, like
> constellations.]

These lines make fun of the decadent atmosphere personified by Darío's Marquesa Eulalia, Proust's world of the Guermantes, and the affectations expressed by these authors' characters. In Huerta's poem there are other references to the emblems of the *modernistas* and the Symbolists, like the swan, the color white, and, in particular, the color blue, which represents, both for Huerta and the turn-of-the-century poets, artistic perfection—"el azul amor" (blue love) (180)—and a poetic transcendence—"asciendo azul, azul, azulmente" (I ascend blue, blue, bluely) (238).

Another parody is this one of César Vallejo—"Yo no sé si Vallejo, yo no sé" (I don't know if Vallejo, I don't know) (324)—which refers to Vallejo's famous "Los Heraldos negros" (The black heralds): "Hay golpes en la vida, tan fuertes . . . Yo no sé" (There are blows in life, so hard . . . I don't know).[15] The next quotation underlines the always doubtful attitude that Huerta's text maintains. These lines, almost borrowed from the doubt-ridden play *Waiting for Godot,* by Samuel Beckett, introduce an attitude of unsureness that increases throughout chapter 8:

> Pues alguien puede llegar, uno de nosotros en toda
> probabilidad.
> Sé hacer algunas cosas, alguien puede llegar, de improviso,
> y borrarlas con su brazo de polvo y entonces
> no sabré ya cuál es mi fiel postura, no sabré quién llegó
> porque alguien puede llegar...
>
> (300)

> [Well, someone may arrive, one of us in all
> probability.
> I know how to do some things, someone may arrive, suddenly,
> and erase them with his arm of dust and then
> I will no longer know which is my faithful position, I will now know
> who arrived
> because someone may arrive . . .]

There are several sections of *Incurable* that recall Alejandra Pizarnik's poetry and also the essays of the French thinker Maurice Blanchot, with the themes of presence/absence and death/night as essential elements for poetry. Here are some of Huerta's lines on those themes:

> que no eras una persona sino la piedra de la muerte, quc tu
> cuerpo florccía en la quemante ausencia...
>
> (200)

> [since you were not a person but rather the stone of death, since
> your body flourished in the burning absence . . .]

En cada vena diurna se deposita una vena nocturna, todo tiene
dos lados y todo lo que está arriba
es igual a todo lo que está abajo...

(229)

[In each daily vein is deposited a nocturnal vein, everything has
two sides and everything is above
it is the same as everything that is below . . .]

Noche, estoy muriendo de ti, solo incurablemente y abandonado.
Noche, delirio. Crece de mí como una rama atroz ya toda mi
alegría,
como de tus espacios la nutritiva forma de mi ausencia.
Ausente, aislado, estoy amarrado a mi sola presencia.

(268)

[Night, I am dying from you, incurably alone and abandoned.
Night, delirium. Now all my happiness grows out of me
like an atrocious branch,
like out of your spaces the nutritious form of my absence.
Absent, isolated, I am tied to my only presence.]

Here are some lines from Pizarnik that are similar to those:

Nadie me conoce yo hablo la noche
nadie me conoce yo hablo mi cuerpo
nadie me conoce yo hablo la lluvia
nadie me conoce yo hablo los muertos.[16]

[No one knows me I speak the night
no one knows me I speak my body
no one knows me I speak the rain
no one knows me I speak the dead.]

en esta noche en este mundo
las palabras del sueño de la infancia de la muerte
. . . .
no
las palabras
no hacen el amor
hacen la ausencia . . .

(67)

[in this night in this world
words of the dream of childhood of death
. . . .
no
words

    don't make love
    they make absence . . .]

There are also references and pastiches of the Bible and of Jorge
Luis Borges, Octavio Paz, José Lezama Lima, and Jorge Guillén,
and surely there are many more. As we already indicated, there
are plays on "telquelism" also, which show both the poet's erudi-
tion and the source of the doubts inherent in all postmodern literature. This next passage refers to serious themes taken from Jacques
Derrida, but it ends with a question that functions as a joke on the
impenetrability of most of the French philosopher's writings.

    No preguntar por la diferencia frente a la puerta de vidrio es
    entrar en la fiesta perversa. La
    puerta de vidrio es el fantasma de toda regularización
    pero también el muro que goza destruyéndose. ¿Has entendido o
        quieres que te lo cuente otra vez?

                                                          (99)

    [Don't ask about difference in front of the glass door since that means
    going into the perverse party. The
    glass door is the phantom of all regularization
    but also the wall that enjoys destroying itself. Have you understood
        or do you want me to tell it to you again?]

Poststructural themes make up "the perverse party," which in
turn recalls Derrida's idea that all writing is a "game": "this field
is really that of a *game,* that is to say of infinite substitutions in
the enclosure of a finite whole."[17] And this game is subject to all
the vicissitudes of the language that goes into any writing. In the
Huerta quote we see the doubt and insecurity that underlie the
game of writing in the phrases "the phantom of all regularization"
and "the wall that enjoys destroying itself." This last one is an
obvious commentary on the theory of "deconstruction" that is
often associated with Derrida.
    These references to some of the texts that make up the author's
own poetic world reveal at the same time both the tensions that
result when poetry turns in on itself and the sense of affirmation
that comes from restating and reformulating texts that have influenced this one. Nevertheless, the subject who speaks is still be-
sieged by doubt, since he rejects the Symbolists' affectations and
shares the literary and artistic burdens so obvious in Vallejo, Pizarnik, and Derrida, especially the latter. But can there not be some
solution for his problem with poetic language? Later in the poem,

the "I" who speaks, after long expressions of dissatisfaction, finds a very simple solution. Because this episode is so important, I quote it in its entirety.

Esto sucede: harto de la retórica al uso, intenté desprenderme
de lo que me oprimía
y el lenguaje se me hizo un gran salón de espejos,
trastabillé, jadeé y puse la mano en la llaga de otro
lenguaje, tremendamente dudé y luego volví la cabeza y
la pluma en la mano
hasta que lo mejor fue ya retroceder, buscar, encontrar para
no desfallecer, al par que la estrella que palidecía dentro
de mi cabeza civilizada.
Retrocedí entonces, me tropecé locamente y luego ascendí por
listas y por montones de palabras. ¿Qué
había de encontrar? No lo sabía, lamí las paredes para buscar
la sal y seguir adelante.
Pero lo que buscaba estaba ahí, seco y desapasionado.
Abrí la boca para decirlo y entonces apareció en mi frente el acuerdo
de mi posible lenguaje con el mundo.
Decidí no desear otra cosa que ese acuerdo pero al entrar en ese
acuerdo
supe que más tarde renunciaría a él. Retrocedía de nuevo y ese retroceder era ya un avance.
Ningún acuerdo, entonces. Mi sola voz lunar bajo las
acumulaciones diurnas.

(278–79)

[This happens: fed up with the usual rhetoric, I tried to get away
from what was getting me down
and language became for me a great hall of mirrors,
I staggered, I gasped, and I stuck my hand in the heart of another
language, I was really doubtful and then I turned my head and the
pen in my hand
until the best thing to do was to move back, look for, and find so I
wouldn't weaken, just like the star that grew pale within
my civilized head.
I went back then, I stumbled wildly and then I climbed up over lists
and over piles of words. What
was I going to find? I didn't know, I licked the walls looking for salt
and kept going.
But what I was looking for was there, dry and dispassionate.
I opened my mouth to say it and then the understanding with my
possible language with the world appeared on my forehead.
I decided not to want anything more than that understanding but
even as I made that agreement

I knew that later on I would renounce it. I moved back again and
   that moving back was now a going forward.
No agreement, then. My single lunar voice under the
daily accumulations.]

The "I" starts out here in a state of insecurity with respect to
language's instability (it was a "hall of mirrors") and at this point
comes across "another language." What it finds are "lists" and
"piles of words," all "dry and dispassionate." The result is an understanding of this new "language with the world," a language in
perfect symmetry with the objects in the world. It is easy to see
this description of an alternative language as similar to the one
that is imagined and proposed by some of the other poets we have
seen, especially Gonzalo Millán with his "objetivismo" and Jorge
Luis Borges with what he called a "language of iron"—in each
case a language magically symbolic of what it represents.
   Our poet rejects the solutions that this idealistically perfect alternative language might provide ("ningún acuerdo entonces"), prefer-
ring instead his former perplexed state: that of a poet confronted
with the problem of representing everyday objects. His only tool
for that purpose is described here as the "single lunar voice," a
term that makes us think of the romantics and the *modernistas*
(especially Leopoldo Lugones's *Lunario sentimental*), and it even
evokes what "lunatics" might sound like, howling at the moon in
their madness. The madness implied by this term is clearly the
result of having rejected a too-perfect "solution" to his very problematic relationship with language, a situation indicated by his reference, in a line not cited, to "my blinded tongue." This hypallage
represents his return to a state in which he cannot reproduce a
language adequate for representing reality, a situation directly acknowledged in these next lines from the poem:

> Un mar la realidad. Su puerto imposible, esa puerta de
> vidrio. Límite ciego bajo las enredadas junturas de la
> materia toda-enorme: mundo innombrable.
>
> (126)

> [A sea, reality. Its impossible port, that glass door.
> A blind limit underneath the tangled joints of
> all-enormous matter: unnameable world.]

This completely unnameable world ("each unnameable frag-
ment," another line says) is one that resolutely resists being represented by language. Even if it could be named, if there could be a

miraculous solution like the one in the previous quote, the poet
would have to reject it, as he did there. Then what? The whole
poem is an answer to this dilemma, and the explanation is scattered
all through the book. For example, let's look at these lines from
early in the poem, which begin with Derridean language:

> Escribir proporciona un desvío, una deriva, incluso una fuga,
> una fuga equívoca que sedimenta más que diseminar, que
> aglomera más que desordenar,
> y reconstruye una imagen donde no hay más que "tratos hechos".
> Reconstruye la imagen porque ya, como figura o perfil, estaba
> esa imagen dentro de la persona: ésta reconoce, en el extravío
> de sí misma,
> el lenguaje total, nebuloso y fincado en la materia de la imagen.
>
> (36)

> [Writing provides a detour, a drifting, even a fleeing,
> a mistaken fugue that sediments more than it disseminates, that
> agglomerates more than it disorders,
> and reconstructs an image where there are only "done deals."
> It reconstructs the image because now, as a figure or profile, it was
> that image within the person: this one recognizes, in the mislaying
> of itself,
> the total, nebulous language lying in the image's matter.]

With a clever play on words ("fuga" means both fleeing and
fugue), writing is here equated with a musical fugue. Fittingly, the
characteristics inherent in both of those textual forms—detour,
drifting, fleeing—coincide with the terminology that Derrida uses
to explain language's instability. But the result here, more than
that "sedimentation," is that writing "reconstructs an image." The
reiteration of this result—"it reconstructs the image"—is important because, as we have often noted, "repetition is itself a
sign." Besides, here there is a doubly strong repetition—in the
phrase itself being duplicated and in the verb *re*construct; the word
"image" also appears four times, augmenting this symbolic effect.
Such textual insistence reinforces the emblematic condition of the
image. A product of desire (it comes from "within the person"),
the image is recognized "in the mislaying of the person"—a process
that recalls all the dialogues that take place between the "you" and
the "I" within the subject throughout the poem. The result is not
a perfect solution: it is a "total language," but also a nebulous one
that resides within the image itself.

If images are really suggested as a solution to the poet's dilemma, then we must try to answer another question. What are the characteristics of the images in Huerta's poetry, and how do they produce a "total" language? The following quote suggests that they follow in the pattern of the intrasubject dialogues and are the result of the dichotomy between presence (memory) and absence (forgetting):

Las imágenes pasan por el anillo de hierro de la memoria y
por el anillo de hierro del olvido.
Pasan fulgurando hacia la mano, hacia el ojo—el cuerpo
se reconstruye en la versión que de sí mismo se da en el
vuelo intocable y llameante de las imágenes produciéndose,
produciéndose sin cesar y sin orilla.

(172)

[The images go through memory's iron ring and
through forgetting's iron ring.
They go shining through my hand, toward my eye—my body
rebuilds itself in the version of itself that comes in the
untouchable and flaming flight of the images producing themselves,
producing themselves endlessly and without containment.]

The effect that these images produce—as they produce themselves—is that of brightness ("shining," "flaming"), a concept that is infinitely repeated throughout the poem. They also offer a way out of the inspirational crisis that recurs throughout the poem, since they come at the poet unbidden ("producing themselves"), constantly ("endlessly"), and unlimitedly ("without containment"). The problems of mimesis and of a language shunted aside and postponed are not automatically eliminated by this image-centered strategy, as various milestones in the history of poetry prove. We only have to think about the poems and manifestos of the avant-garde in the 1920s to see the fallacy inherent in the idea of basing everything on image and metaphor. But in this text images represent *one* answer—total but nebulous—that indeed allows the poet to surpass the limits imposed by rationality. As we said, it is a solution that is literally "brilliant," with the images having just such a glowing effect.

Una palabra le quema, sus letras arden contra la noche
blanca y silenciosa de la página: esta ceniza puesta en
mi boca.

(45)

[A word burns him, its letters burn against the white
and silent night of the page: this ash placed in
my mouth.]

With this burning image, the text metaphorically represents the
desired transcendent effect. But only desired. The poet who speaks
is aware of all the realities, all the problems, but still proposes
poetry as a solution, as long as it allows those images to burn
against the page. The end of the poem, however, does not boast
about this solution. To the contrary: in what the text says is its
"anticlimax," we see good evidence of humor, resignation, and
willpower as the poet presents a sort of Borgesian disclaimer, or
admission of fallibility, in the face of reality. The subject once again
admits to the difficulty of his undertaking, of trying to describe all
the problems that come with poetic discourse, and of having to do
so in a language by nature defective. But he does it with humor,
in full knowledge of the irony behind his efforts.

Ya voy a terminar, espero se me escuche. ¿Se me escucha?
Estoy haciendo una serie de piruetas ridículas
para que se me escuche.

(382)

[Now I'm going to end, I hope I'm being heard. Is anyone listening?
I'm doing a series of ridiculous piruettes
so I'll be heard.]

Knowing the difficulties that certainly lie in the way of transmitting
his ideas by means of language, and writing "in poetry," the subject
gets desperate (or pretends to get desperate) here. The "ridiculous
piruettes" that he does are indeed absurd, if the theoretical problems are really not solvable. Conscious that the "solution" that he
has presented is only one possible answer, the poet recognizes that
the dilemmas continue. Now he addresses poetry:

. . . navío ya totalmente deshecho, poesía. Es
el sabor de los derrotados, la incruenta lastimadura
de los heroicos y la embriaguez de los sobrios.
Es el delirio encima de la piel afinada hasta el martirio.
Esto he escrito, dicho, declamado, sangrado:

Lo que describo ahora es una imperfección, mis lentitudes, rayas
que el silencio del mundo no le dio al amor.

(383)

[. . . a ship now totally undone, poetry. It is
the taste of the defeated, the bloodless injury
of the heroic ones and the drunkenness of the sober.
It is delirium on top of skin polished to the point of martyrdom.
This I have written, said, declaimed, bled:

What I describe now is an imperfection, my slownesses, lines
that the world's silence did not give to love.]

All the contradictions come out in these lines. Poetry is an "undone ship"; it is deconstructed, discredited. Full of contradictions,
poetry is for both the heroic and the defeated. It can intoxicate
sober people, and it is the ecstasy that comes from the martyr's
suffering. All of these incongruences make sense in the context of
this poem, as a review of its basic arguments should help to make
clear. Rationally, we have to recognize the validity of the poem's
arguments that place in doubt the function of language, and of
poetry. Still, we must take into account that the doubt that comes
out of these poststructuralist concepts—such as the instability of
the sign, the contradictions that are always to be found in texts,
the deconstruction inherent in the reading process—results, paradoxically, in a completely open poem that implies the appearance
of a limitless text. Also, poetry may, in spite of its recognized
difficulties, intoxicate its readers and dazzle them with the transcendent effect of the shining poetic image—in this way detouring
around poetry's rational limits. In short, what the poet describes
is indeed an "imperfection." It is not a perfect solution, but a
poetry filled with images that can effectively provide momentary
transcendence is preferable to the alternative "language of the
world": a static "list" of words linked to the objects that they
describe.

This rather flat summary of the phenomenological explication
that emanates from *Incurable* is, to be sure, prosaic and mundane,
but it can only be that way. Huerta's text is infinitely richer than
any reconstruction of the text's underlying ideas could possibly
be, precisely because all of its argumentations in favor of the power
of the image are made *with* images.[18]

As an overtly critical poem, *Incurable* gives a wonderful demonstration of the open functioning of the text in this postmodern age.
And it suggests a way possibly to move beyond the openly "critical" stage. Specifically, it is very possible that this book's greatest
value is that it rescues, and revalues, the image. Throughout this
text, with all its evocations of the problems that besiege the poetic

text, *Incurable* proposes the image as a valid response to the dilemma, if not the crisis, of critical poetry. In short:

> Hay una libertad, hay un deseo. Veo mi rostro, sigo.
> Camino hasta donde no sé. Todo lo que yo sé está aquí,
> todo confuso, algebraico, en poesía . . .

(387)

> [There is a freedom, there is a desire. I see my face, I go on.
> I walk to I don't know where. All I know is here,
> all confused, algebraic, in poetry . . .]

What is important is that the poet who speaks goes on "in poetry," in images. He is not limited by the goal of trying to represent reality, a goal now discarded. He says that everything is "confused," that he does not know where he is going. But that is part of the answer. Because he has rejected that stable, too-perfect "language of the world," he has a new freedom. Now the poet can try to transcend the rational limits of poetry by means of the poetic image.

The very last section of *Incurable* would seem to support this idea, as it presents a somewhat confused demonstration of image and inspiration—and of inspiration through image. Even here at the end of the long poem, though, there is this one last recalling of how the poet was affected by an awareness of poetry's limits:

> Qué limites ardieron por aquí, por estas manos, esta
> boca, estas cadencias de escribir.

(386)

> [What limits burned here, in these hands, this
> mouth, these cadences of writing.]

But, a few lines later, there is this strong recognition of desire and of its hold on the writer, which also underlines how desire has an essential role in overcoming the paralysis that the limits might have caused.

> Se despeña uno en las ganas de seguir escribiendo . . .

> [One throws oneself into the desire to keep writing . . .]

Then the final two dense pages present a rather surrealistic series of images that describe the poet-subject's view of what he "has to write." Here are a few of these verses:

Alzo la cara, veo espejos . . .
Veo la llamarada, las rayas doradas en movimiento.

. . . .
Me levanto, dudo de todo.
Me entrego a la luz, otra vez me levanto. El mundo
es una mancha en el espejo. La luz va dándome nombre,
        no lo quiero.
El mundo me dice lo que tiene que ser. Hay una llama viva.
Tendré que decir lo que tenga que decir—o callarme.

                                                    (389)

[I raise my head, I see mirrors . . .
I see the flame, the golden rays in movement.

. . . .
I get up, I doubt everything.
I give myself up to the light, again I get up. The world
is a stain on the mirror. The light is giving me a name,
        I don't like it.
The world tells me what has to be. There is a living flame.
I'll have to say what I have to say—or be silent.]

Truly lighting the way, these "brilliant," shining, light-filled images are here presenting themselves as both source of inspiration
and as a means of poetic expression that would not be bound by the
previously bothersome limits. The prominent references to mirrors
emphasize the importance of both the visual and the repetitive
functions of the image for the poet. But the tensions with the
world—the rational approach to representing "reality"—are still
causing confusion for the speaker in the poem right up to the end.
There, in the very last line, we notice a clearly resigned tone. But
he *is* saying, continuing to write. What he is writing about, significantly, is what he is being given: the brilliant images. The speaker
is not able to simply accept these shining moments of inspiration,
though. He is still being a self-conscious, critical writer, insisting
on simultaneously acknowledging his confusion and doubt at the
rational level.

Huerta's text certainly practices what it preaches. Its images,
as we have said, demonstrate the same critical concepts that they
themselves are describing. Used in this extremely self-conscious
manner, they also in no way go against the guiding principles of
the "critical poem." In fact, as *Incurable* demonstrates, the image
that is capable of provoking an intense, readerly reaction is the
most effective, and maybe the only way of getting around the limitations that the critical poet sees so clearly. But, this being a critical

poem, nothing can be stated as a certainty. Perhaps for this reason, in *Incurable,* the final images do not do away with doubt altogether.

Although the other critical poets that we have studied have not overtly presented the image as a possible solution to the dilemmas that they have encountered, we have seen the image used with remarkable effectiveness in their poetry also. Now, with the focus that Huerta's text places on the image as a possible remedy to poetry's postmodern ills, we can, in the conclusion, briefly look back at how the image coexists with the critical concepts the other poets have been dealing with.

Conclusion

MAYBE the critical poem can be looked at as similar to the photographic process, where we use the negative to get a positive picture. Many of the poems we have discussed give us what looks like a negative, reverse view of the poetic process. But despite all the criticism that we have seen aimed at poetry's own ability to say or be anything meaningful, despite the fact that all of this criticism is contained *within the texts* of these poems themselves, despite the complete rejection of a traditional view of language that these poems present, these poems are fully focused and developed literary texts. They are still being given form by language. And they are still saying something—a great deal, in fact. But some of that *saying* has come about through *showing*.

In the final chapter we saw the use of the poetic image in David Huerta's long poem, both as a poetic device in its own right and as a means of transcending what the critical poets often seem to see as a "failed" language. Huerta is the only one of our critical poets to so explicitly display and expose the image as one possible solution to the impasse that these poets have created for themselves with their critique of language. But we have also seen various uses of this device in the other poets. Gonzalo Millán gives us words seen as taxis filled with letters and the white page pictured as hard-frozen snow. Juan Luis Martínez uses real images: fishhooks and flags, as well as pictures, drawings, and graphs. And Octavio Paz, a virtuoso with the words that he professes to have so little faith in, whips up his "spirals of echoes." Even Roberto Juarroz—the advocate of "desnombrar," or unnaming—whose texts present such a strong case for a sign stripped of its signifieds, sometimes uses images to outline his poetic philosophies.[1]

In fact, I would now like to look back at an early Juarroz poem to show that even when most of his texts were presenting a rather stark view of both language and poetic possibilities, that message was being presented by poems composed of rather gripping images. This is poem number 10, from Juarroz's first *Poesía vertical*.

177

Hallé un hombre escribiendo en sus huesos
y yo, que nunca he visto un Dios,
sé que ese hombre se parece a un Dios.

Había en su gesto algo
equivalente a la norma o el olor del suicida,
un abismo o un silencio
que divide al universo en dos partes, exactas y nocturnas.

Escribía en sus huesos
como en la arena de una playa horadada desde arriba
y con la integridad de un ojo
que encerrara en sí mismo también al pensamiento.

Pero no pude mirar sobre su hombro
para ver qué escribía,
porque también en su hombro escribía.[2]

[I found a man writing on his bones
and I, who have never seen a God,
know that that man looks like a God.

There was in his manner something
like the norm or odor of the suicidal,
an abyss or a silence
that divides the universe into two exact and nocturnal parts.

He was writing on his bones
as if on the sand of a beach pierced from above
and with the integrity of an eye
that also encloses thought within itself.

But I couldn't look over his shoulder
to see what he was writing,
because he was also writing on his shoulder.]

Rather than the stark texts usually associated with Juarroz, this actually looks, at first reading, like a Surrealist dreamlike description. To see a man writing would certainly be a normal occurrence, but to see him writing "on his bones" gives us an unusual picture. There may well be an underlying semantic explanation (what Michael Riffaterre would call a "hypogram") for this action, and in this case the underlying element is a cliché. We can either see the man the text is describing as one who is steeped in writing "hasta los huesos" or, in English, as a man who has "writing in his bones." And such a man, to take one more short interpretive step, is almost by definition a poet. This poet, with "writing in his bones," is represented as "looking like" a god.

And poets have long been associated with divinely inspired creation, a process culminating, of course, in Vicente Huidobro's famous verse from his "Arte poética": "el poeta es un pequeño Dios" (the poet is a small God). In any case we now have a double image, or picture, of the man writing on himself and looking like a god. In the second strophe we have a godlike action—a gesture that divides the universe in two. This is another image, a large one both in scope and in what it suggests. The division into "two exact and nocturnal parts" parallels the life/death and presence/absence tensions that determine Alejandra Pizarnik's poetry, as well as that of David Huerta. But here those larger issues are just suggested by the single picture of the godlike hand stroke and the opposing structures it creates.

The third stanza begins by repeating the poem's first image—of the poet-god writing on his bones. But now that picture is compared to another one—the sands of a beach being drilled through from above. This can either refer to the abyss of suicide in the prior stanza—the poet's own mortality is seen as the sands of his time eroding—or it can show the futility of his writing, as it is chipped away. This second reading of the image is similar to the effect produced by the Gonzalo Millán poem where the futility of writing is pictured as the impossibility of making a dent on the frozen snow. The final image in this stanza, that of the eye that encloses all thought, reinforces the effect produced by the poet's writing being done on (or in) himself. The integrity attributed to this action must refer to the self-consciousness of this activity, as well as to its self-contained purpose: all of the effort is going *into* the writing.

We return to the first-person voice of the poem in the last stanza, where he realizes that even though he has been looking at a picture of the writing process, that picture can reveal only so much. The "I" who has been witnessing all of the action ("I found," "I have never seen," "I couldn't look"), after the expanded description of poetry that the text has presented (at its deeper level of "significance"), is finally closed out of the process.

Any poet could explain this final irony. Poetry, or its inspiration, is a closed process: it is not self-revealing even to its maker. And this poem, on the narrative level, is its own highly specific example of this paradox. Even though the poet within the poem here is constructing this specific poem, he still cannot "see into," or understand, his source of creation. Almost exactly as it happened in

David Huerta's *Incurable,* this poem does tell us what is necessary in order to "make" a good poet, however. He has to have writing in his bones. This means, as we also saw in Huerta's long poem, that the poet has to have the poetic process completely thought through. Such a saturation with poetry can lead to a "writerly" text that both internalizes and exposes its own propensity for failure. In this way the poem's own structure and its underpinnings have now become visible within a transparent text, somewhat comparable to a Marcel Duchamp work of art enclosed within several panes of glass. So it is now possible to look *through* the text, into and then past its opposing structures, and then back into the text, where the process could begin again—thought "enclosed within itself," as the Juarroz poem put it. It is important to note that in this process the opposing structures, rather than canceling themselves out, form an intertwining, intermittent tension that puts the text into motion.

We can see this happening in the Juarroz poem above. The "I" in the text is clearly looking inside the poem, seeing how it develops itself (the poet-god writing on his bones). But he is not able to see the process come to an end, because the process is continuous—the poet-god is now writing on his shoulder, and the viewer in the text even *says* he cannot see beyond that.

There we have the basic image that all of these critical poets have left us. With all their failures, opposing forces, and resulting inner tensions exposed, their texts open up to reveal the poem at work.

Notes

Chapter 1. The Critical Poem

1. Octavio Paz, *Alternating Current,* trans. Helen R. Lane (New York: Viking, 1973), 3–5. The sentences I comment on, in their original Spanish, follow: "El poema no tiene objeto o referencia exterior; la referencia de una palabra es otra palabra . . . el sentido no está fuera sino dentro del poema: no en lo que dicen las palabras, sino en aquello que *se dicen entre ellas.* . . . En Rimbaud y en Mallarmé el lenguaje se interioriza, cesa de designar y no es símbolo ni mención de realidades externas, trátese de objetos físicos o suprasensibles. . . . La palabra es el reverso de la realidad: no la nada sino la idea, el signo puro que ya no designa y que no es ni ser ni no-ser" (Octavio Paz, *Corriente alterna* [Mexico City: Siglo Veintiuno Editores, 1967], 5–7).

2. Gerald Bruns, *Modern Poetry and the Idea of Language* (New Haven: Yale University Press, 1974).

3. Jonathan Mayhew, *Claudio Rodríguez and the Language of Poetic Vision* (Lewisburg, Pa.: Bucknell University Press, 1990), 19.

4. Michael Riffaterre, in a talk given at Princeton University in July 1981.

5. Marjorie Perloff, in *The Poetics of Indeterminacy* (Princeton: Princeton University Press, 1981), surveys certain modern poets, such as Ezra Pound, Gertrude Stein, and John Ashbery, whom she sees as following the lead of Rimbaud. In contrast to Mallarmé, who presented a meaning below the surface of his texts, these poets concentrate on playing with language on the surface. They resist what Perloff calls a "fixity," refusing to "mean in conventional ways" (34). By using language in unconventional ways they may imply a skeptical view of language, but they do not express an open distrust of it, as do the critical poets, whom Paz sees as following Mallarmé's lead.

6. Christopher Norris, *Deconstruction: Theory and Practice* (New York: Methuen, 1982), 24.

7. Stéphane Mallarmé, *Oeuvres complètes* (Paris: Gallimard, 1945), 457–77. Translation by myself and Ned Dubin. All other translations to English are mine, unless otherwise attributed.

8. Jacques Derrida, *Of Grammatology,* trans. Gayatri Spivak (Baltimore: Johns Hopkins University Press, 1976), 74.

9. Paul de Man, *Allegories of Reading* (New Haven: Yale University Press, 1979), 17.

10. Robert Greer Cohn, *Mallarmé's Divagations* (New York: Peter Lang, 1990), 59.

11. Octavio Paz, "Signs in Rotation," in *The Bow and the Lyre,* trans. Ruth L. C. Simms (Austin: University of Texas Press, 1973), 250. ("Poema crítico: si no me equivoco, la unión de estas dos palabras contradictorias quiere decir: aquel poema que contiene su propia negación y que hace de esa negación el punto de

181

partida del canto, a igual distancia de afirmación. La poesía . . . se niega a sí misma cada vez que se realiza en un poema . . . salvo si el poema es simultáneamente crítica de esa tentativa. La negación de la negación anula el absurdo y disuelve el azar": Octavio Paz, *Los signos en rotación y otros ensayos* [Madrid: Alianza Editorial, 1971], 326). Mallarmé uses the term "le poème critique" in the detailed biographical notes he provided for *Divagations*, as Gordon Millan indicates in his book *A Throw of the Dice: The Life of Stéphane Mallarmé* (New York: Farrar, Straus and Giroux, 1994), 309.

12. Jaime Siles, *Poesía 1969–1990* (Madrid: Visor, 1992), 190.
13. Andrew P. Debicki, *Poetry of Discovery* (Lexington: University of Kentucky Press, 1982).
14. Juan Ramón Jiménez, *Segunda antolojía poética* (Madrid: Espasa-Calpe, 1987), 236.
15. Ibid., 122.
16. Gerardo Diego, *Antología poética* (Madrid: Ministerio de Educación y Ciencia, 1969), 13.
17. Guillermo Sucre, *La máscara, la transparencia* (Mexico City: Fondo de Cultura Económica, 1985), 225–34.
18. Jean Franco, "La temática de *Los heraldos negros* a los 'Poemas póstumos,' in César Vallejo, *Obra poética,* critical edition coordinated by Américo Ferrari (Paris: Archivos, 1988), 575–605 (these quotes, 604).
19. César Vallejo, *Obra poética* (Paris: Archivos, 1988), 352.
20. Ibid., 400.
21. Roberto Juarroz, *Poesía y creación: diálogos con Guillermo Boido* (Buenos Aires: Carlos Lohlé, 1980), 117.
22. Vicente Huidobro, *Obras completas* (Santiago: Editorial Andrés Bello, 1976), 219, 341.
23. Ibid., 498.
24. René de Costa, *Vicente Huidobro: The Careers of a Poet* (Oxford: Clarendon Press, 1984), 147–54.
25. Huidobro, *Obras completas,* 382.

Chapter 2. Octavio Paz and the Magic of the Word

1. Octavio Paz, *Alternating Current,* 51 (hereafter cited in the text as *AC*).
2. Jason Wilson, *Octavio Paz: A Study of His Poetics* (London: Cambridge University Press, 1979).
3. Alejandra Pizarnik, "El premio internacional de pocsía: *Salamandra,*" in *Octavio Paz,* ed. Pere Gimferrer (Madrid: Taurus, 1982), 199.
4. Saúl Yurkiévich, "Octavio Paz, indagador de la palabra," in *Octavio Paz,* ed. Gimferrer, 106.
5. Octavio Paz, *Libertad bajo palabra* (Mexico City: Fondo de Cultura Económica, 1960), 31–32.
6. Lelia Madrid, "Octavio Paz: la invención del origen," *Insula* 46, no. 532–35 (April-May 1991): 27–28.
7. Octavio Paz, *Pasado en claro* (Mexico City: FCE, 1978), 39.
8. Octavio Paz, *Salamandra* (Mexico City: Joaquín Mortiz, 1962), 31.
9. José Miguel Oviedo, "Los pasos de la memoria," *Revista de occidente* 14 (1976): 42–44, 51.

10. Manuel Durán, "La huella del Oriente en la poesía de Octavio Paz," in *Octavio Paz* ed. Gimferrer, (Madrid: Taurus, 1982), 236–53.

11. Paz, *Pasado en claro,* 10. Subsequent quotations from this work are cited in the text.

12. Julia Kushigian, *Orientalism in the Hispanic Literary Tradition* (Albuquerque: University of New Mexico Press, 1991), 44.

13. Octavio Paz, *Conjunctions and Disjunctions,* trans. Helen R. Lane (New York: Viking, 1974), 59–65.

14. Octavio Paz, *The Bow and the Lyre,* 14.

15. Octavio Paz, *Arbol adentro* (Barcelona: Seix Barral, 1987), 166.

Chapter 3. Roberto Juarroz: Exploding the Limits

1. Roberto Juarroz, *Poesía y creación: diálogos con Guillermo Boido* (Buenos Aires: Carlos Lohlé, 1980), 93.

2. Ibid., 48.

3. Roberto Juarroz, *Poesía vertical* (Caracas: Monte Avila, 1976), 36. The first through the sixth collections titled *Poesía vertical* are included in this volume. Further references to poems from collections one to six are from this publication and are cited by page number in the text.

4. Jacques Derrida, *L'écriture et la différance* (Paris: Editions du Seuil, 1967). This and the next two Derrida citations are from pages 409–11.

5. Roberto Juarroz, *Novena poesía vertical y décima poesía vertical* (Buenos Aires: Carlos Lohlé, 1986), 66.

6. Maurice Blanchot, *L'espace littéraire* (Paris: Gallimard, 1955), 52.

7. Derrida, *L'ecriture,* 45.

8. François Rigolot, "Le poétique et l'analogique," in *Sémantique de la poésie,* ed. T. Todorov et al. (Paris: Editions du Seuil, 1979), 174.

9. Blanchot, *L'espace Littéraire,* 18.

10. Ibid., 17.

11. Octavio Paz, *Los hijos del limo* (Barcelona: Seix Barral, 1974), 109.

12. Jorge Rodríguez Padrón, "La aventura poética de Roberto Juarroz," *Nueva estafeta* 54 (1983): 47–54.

13. Juarroz, *Novena poesía vertical y décima poesía vertical,* 36–37.

14. Roberto Juarroz, *Undécima poesía vertical* (Valencia: Pre-textos, 1988), 125.

15. Ibid., 141.

16. Jeffrey T. Nealon, "The Discipline of Deconstruction," *PMLA* 107, no. 5 (October 1992): 1270.

Chapter 4. *The New Novel* by Juan Luis Martínez

1. The premature death of this gracious man was due to complications from the diabetes that he had lived with for years.

2. Rudolf Arnheim, *The Image and the Eye* (Ithaca: Cornell University Press, 1982), 296.

3. Santiago Daydí-Tolson, "La obra de Juan Luis Martínez: un ejemplo de poética chilena actual," *Romance Languages Annual,* 3 (1991): 406–10. Jack Schmitt, Martínez's translator to English, goes so far as to call *La nueva novela*

"expansive multimedia probings" ("From *The New Novel,*" *Review,* no. 49 [Fall 1994]: 71–83).

4. Rudolf Arnheim, *New Essays on the Psychology of Art* (Berkeley: University of California Press, 1986), 17.

5. Enrique Lihn and Pedro Lastra, *Señales de ruta de Juan Luis Martínez* (Santiago de Chile: Ediciones archivo, 1987). ("a todas las artes cuyo lenguaje no es literalmente descifrable: la pintura, la música . . .), 16.

6. Kevin Barry, cited in Christopher Norris, *What's Wrong with Postmodernism* (Baltimore: Johns Hopkins University Press, 1991), 207. Norris discusses Barry's book *Language, Music and the Sign: A Study of Aesthetics, Poetics and Poetic Practice from Collins to Coleridge* (Cambridge: Cambridge University Press, 1987).

7. Daydí-Tolson's study of *La nueva novela* centers on how the book's cover relates to the work as a whole.

8. Alain Robbe-Grillet, *For a New Novel,* translated by Richard Howard (New York: Grove Press, 1965).

9. Wolfgang Iser, "Interaction between Text and Reader," in *The Reader in the Text,* ed. Susan R. Suleiman and Inge Crossman (Princeton: Princeton University Press, 1980), 106.

10. Juan Luis Martínez, *La nueva novela* (Santiago: Ediciones Archivo, 1985; facsimile edition of the first edition of 1977), 58.

11. Jaime Valdivieso, "El contra-universo entre las páginas de un libro," *La Época* (Chile), 11 September 1988, "Literatura y libros," 3.

12. Eduardo Stilman, *El libro del humor absurdo* (Buenos Aires: Ediciones Siglo Veinte, 1977), 130–34.

13. María Ester Roblero Cum, "Juan Luis Martínez: 'Me complace irradiar una identidad velada,'" *El Mercurio,* no. 202: (14 March 1993), "Revista de Libros" 1, 4–5.

14. Lihn and Lastra, *Señales de ruta,* 15–16.

15. Roblero Cum, "Juan Luis Martínez," 4 ("Desgraciadamente, desde cierto punto de vista, soy un poeta manipulador de significantes").

16. Ibid., 5.

17. Michael Riffaterre, *Semiotics of Poetry* (Bloomington: University of Indiana Press, 1978), 49.

Chapter 5. The Negative Poems of Alejandra Pizarnik

1. Alejandra Pizarnik, *Obras completas* (Buenos Aires: Corregidor, 1991), 64 (hereafter cited as *OC* in the text).

2. Perla Schwartz, *El quebranto del silencio: mujeres suicidas del siglo XX* (Mexico City: Editorial Diana, 1989), 97.

3. Inés Malinow, "Juicios críticos," in *Poesía argentina contemporánea* (Buenos Aires: Fundación argentina para la poesía, 1980), 2833–40. Malinow gives relatively intimate details of Pizarnik's life and work, in large part based on the poet's own diaries.

4. For a more detailed study of the connections between painting and Pizarnik's poetry, see Carlota Caulfield, "Entre la poesía y la pintura: elementos surrealistas en *Extracción de la piedra de locura* y *El infierno musical* de Alejandra Pizarnik," *Chasqui,* 21, no. 1 (May 1992): 3–10.

5. Alejandra Pizarnik, *La última inocencia y Las aventuras perdidas* (Buenos Aires: Botella al Mar, 1976), 24.

6. Octavio Paz, "The image," in *The Bow and the Lyre*, 86–87.

7. Michael Riffaterre, *Semiotics of Poetry* (Bloomington: University of Indiana Press, 1978), 19.

8. Pizarnik, *La última inocencia y Las aventuras perdidas*, 44. (hereafter cited as *Aventuras* in the text).

9. Alejandra Pizarnik, "El poeta y su poema," in *Antología consultada de la joven poesía argentina* (Buenos Aires: Fabril Editora, 1968), 67.

10. Jurii Lotman, *Analysis of the Poetic Text* (Ann Arbor, Mich.: Ardis, 1978), 85.

11. Riffaterre, *Semiotics*, 19.

12. Maurice Blanchot, *L'espace littéraire* (Paris: Gallimard, 1955), 107.

13. Jonathan Culler, *On Deconstruction* (Ithaca: Cornell University Press, 1982), 95.

14. Blanchot, *L'espace*, 215.

15. Marta Moia, interview with Alejandra Pizarnik, in Alejandra Pizarnik, *El deseo de la palabra* (Barcelona: Ocnos, 1975), 249.

16. Blanchot, *L'espace*, 216, 26.

17. Ibid., 27–28.

18. Pizarnik, "El poeta y su poema," 67.

Chapter 6. Alberto Girri: Poetry about Poetry

1. Enrique Pezzoni, interview with Girri, in Alberto Girri, *Obra poética*, vol. 4 (Buenos Aires: Corregidor, 1984), 153.

2. Ibid, 153.

3. Alberto Girri, *Páginas de Alberto Girri* (Buenos Aires: Editorial Sudamericana, 1986), 72–73. (hereafter cited in text as *P*).

4. Murray S. Krieger, *Words about Words about Words* (Baltimore: Johns Hopkins University Press, 1988), 108.

5. Ibid., 66.

6. Enrique Pezzoni, *El texto y sus voces* (Buenos Aires: Editorial Sudamericana, 1986), 103.

7. Krieger, *Words*, 198.

8. Alberto Girri, *Existenciales* (Buenos Aires: Editorial Sudamericana, 1986), 27-30. (hereafter cited in text as *E*).

9. Alberto Girri, *Monodias* (Buenos Aires: Editorial Sudamericana, 1985), 43–44.

10. Alberto Girri, *Tramas de conflictos* (Buenos Aires: Editorial Sudamericana, 1988), 17.

11. Krieger, *Words*, 110.

Chapter 7. The "Secret Complexity" of Jorge Luis Borges's Poetry

1. Emir Rodríguez Monegal, "Borges y la 'nouvelle critique,'" in *Jorge Luis Borges*, ed. Jaime Alazraki (Madrid: Taurus, 1976), 267–87. See also Emir Rodríguez Monegal, "Borges and Derrida Apothecaries," in *Borges and His Successors*, ed. Edna Aizenberg, (Columbia: University of Missouri Press, 1990), 128–38.

2. Arturo Echavarría, *Lengua y literatura de Borges* (Barcelona: Editorial Ariel, 1983), 30–32.

3. Sylvia Molloy, "'Dios acecha en los intervalos': simulacro y causalidad textual en la ficción de Borges," *Revista Iberoamericana* 100–101 (July-December 1977): 139.

4. Jorge Luis Borges, *Obra poética (1923–1977)* (Buenos Aires: Emecé, 1977), 557. All references in the text to Borges's poetry are from this volume, unless otherwise indicated.

5. Sylvia Molloy, *Signs of Borges,* trans. Oscar Montero and Sylvia Molloy (Durham, N.C.: Duke University Press, 1994), 89.

6. Jacques Derrida, *L'écriture et la différance* (Paris: Editions du Seuil, 1967), 411.

7. Jacques Derrida, *Positions* (Paris: Les Editions de Minuit, 1972), 40.

8. Roman Jakobson, *Lingüística, poética, tiempo* (Barcelona: Editorial Crítica, 1981), p, 97.

9. Jorge Luis Borges, *La cifra* (Madrid: Alianza Tres, 1981), 47. The reference to archetypes here is not a casual one. In *La cifra* Borges repeatedly brings up the notion of a Platonic ideal; it seems obvious that he would like to extend the return to original linguistic symbols all the way back to an archetype.

10. Jorge Luis Borges, *El otro, el mismo* (Buenos Aires: Emecé, 1969), 10.

11. Jorge Luis Borges, *Los conjurados* (Madrid: Alianza Editorial, 1985), 11.

12. Borges, *El otro, el mismo,* 74.

13. Françoise Collin, "From Blanchot to Borges," in *Borges and His Successors,* ed. Aizenberg, 91.

Chapter 8. Gonzalo Millán and "Objective Poetry"

1. Gonzalo Millán, "Hacia la objetividad," in *Entre la lluvia y el arcoiris (Antología de jóvenes poetas chilenos),* ed. Soledad Bianchi (Rotterdam: Ediciones del Instituto para el Nuevo Chile, 1983), 57.

2. Daniel Freidemberg, "Gonzalo Millán," *Diario de la poesía,* Winter 1991, 28–29.

3. Gonzalo Millán, *Relación personal* (Santiago: Arancibia Hermanos, 1968).

4. Carmen Foxley, "La negatividad productiva y los gajes del oficio. La poesía de Gonzalo Millán," in Carmen Foxley and Ana María Cúneo, *Seis poetas de los sesenta* (Santiago de Chile: Editorial Universitaria, 1991), 54–86.

5. Foxley and Cúneo, *Seis poetas de los sesenta;* Thorpe Running, "Responses to the Politics of Oppression by Poets in Argentina and Chile," *Hispania* Vol. 73, No. 1 (March 1990): 40–49.

6. Millán, "Hacia la objetividad," 53.

7. Foxley and Cúneo, *Seis poetas de los sesenta,* 78.

8. Gonzalo Millán, *La ciudad* (Ottawa: Les Editions Maison Culturelle Québec-Amérique Latine, 1979), 9–10.

9. Faride Zeran, "La sobredosis de Gonzalo Millán," *La Epoca,* 28 August 1994, "Literatura libros," 4–5.

10. Gonzalo Millán, *Virus* (Santiago: Ediciones Ganymedes, 1987), 15. Subsequent references to this work are cited parenthetically in the text.

11. Gonzalo Millán, unpublished essay, 1991.

Chapter 9. David Huerta: *Incurable*

1. David Huerta, *El jardín de la luz* (Mexico City: UNAM, 1972).
2. Maureen Ahern, "La poesía de David Huerta," *Eco* 255 (January 1983): 248–69.
3. Raquel Barreda Villarreal, "David Huerta," *Vogue* (Mexico City), November 1988, 189–90.
4. David Huerta, *Cuaderno de noviembre* (Mexico City: Alacena/Era, 1976), 27. Subsequent references are cited in the text.
5. David Huerta, *Versión* (Mexico City: Fondo de Cultura Económica, 1978), 49. Subsequent references are cited in the text.
6. David Huerta, *Incurable* (Mexico City: Era, 1987), 3.
7. Reyes, Juan Jose, "David Huerta: curar las pasiones tristes," *El semanario,* 11 October 1987, 5.
8. Jacques Derrida, *L'ecriture et la différence* (Paris: Editions du Seuil, 1967), 410.
9. Jacques Derrida, *Positions* (Paris: Les Editions du Minuit, 1972), 17.
10. Shoshana Felman, *Jacques Lacan and the Adventure of Insight* (Cambridge: Harvard University Press, 1987), 144.
11. Jacques Lacan, *Ecrits I* (Paris: Editions du Seuil, 1966), 14.
12. Felman, *Jacques Lacan,* 123; Lacan, *Ecrits I,* 143.
13. Jacques Derrida, *De la grammatologie* (Paris: Les Editions de Minuit, 1967), 347.
14. Manuel Gutiérrez Nájera, "Mis enlutadas," in *Literatura hispanoamericana,* vol 2, ed. Enrique Anderson-Imbert and Eugenio Florit, (New York: Holt, Rinehart and Winston, 1970), 63.
15. César Vallejo, *Poesía completa* (Mexico City: Premiá Editora, 1983), 25.
16. Alejandra Pizarnik, *Textos de sombra y otros poemas* (Buenos Aires: Editorial Sudamericana, 1982), 62.
17. Derrida, *L'écriture,* 423.
18. At least one critic, however, sees *Incurable* as incarnating "one of the dead ends of modernity" (see Aurelio Asiain, "*Incurable* de David Huerta," *Vuelta* 138 [May 1988]: 50–53).

Conclusion

1. Joaquín Marco says that Juarroz's "search for the essential" limits his use of the image "to the minimum" ("Poesía vertical. Antología," *ABC Literario* 35 [10 July 1992]: 8). It does look that way in some of his poems. In a recent essay, however, almost as if to help validate this concluding chapter, Juarroz states that contemporary poetry has two great resources, "the formidable power of human imagination and its great product that is the image" (el formidable poder de la imaginación humana y su gran producto que es la imagen). (Roberto Juarroz, "Aproximaciones a la poesía moderna," *El Jabalí,* no. 3 [1994]: 6).
2. Roberto Juarroz, *Poesía vertical (1958–1975)* (Caracas: Monte Avila, 1976), 18.

Works Cited

General Works

Anderson-Imbert, Enrique, and Eugenio Florit, eds. *Literatura hispanoamericana*. Vol. 2. New York: Holt, Rinehart and Winston, 1970.

Arnheim, Rudolf. *The Image and the Eye*. Ithaca: Cornell University Press, 1982.

———. *New Essays on the Psychology of Art*. Berkeley: University of California Press, 1986.

Blanchot, Maurice. *L'espace littéraire*. Paris: Gallimard, 1955.

Bruns, Gerald. *Modern Poetry and the Idea of Language*. New Haven: Yale University Press, 1974.

Cohn, Robert Greer. *Mallarmé's Divagations*. New York: Peter Lang, 1990.

Costa, René de. *Vicente Huidobro: The Careers of a Poet*. Oxford: Clarendon Press,1984.

Culler, Jonathan. *On Deconstruction*. Ithaca: Cornell University Press, 1982.

Debicki, Andrew. *Poetry of Discovery*. Lexington: University of Kentucky Press, 1982.

de Man, Paul. *Allegories of Reading*. New Haven: Yale University Press, 1979.

Derrida, Jacques. *L'écriture et la différance*. Paris: Editions du Seuil, 1967.

———. *De la grammatologie*. Paris: Les Editions de Minuit, 1967.

———. *Of Grammatology*. Translated by Gayatri Spivak. Baltimore: Johns Hopkins University Press, 1976.

———. *Positions*. Paris: Les Éditions de Minuit, 1972.

Diego, Gerardo. *Antología poética*. Madrid: Ministerio de Educación y Ciencia, 1969.

Felman, Shoshana. *Jacques Lacan and the Adventure of Insight*. Cambridge: Harvard University Press, 1987.

Franco, Jean, "La temática de *Los heraldos negros* a los 'Poemas póstumos'." In César Vallejo, *Obra poética*, critical edition coordinated by Américo Ferrari, 575–605. Paris: Archivos, 1988.

Huidobro, Vicente. *Obras completas*. Santiago: Editorial Andrés Bello, 1976.

Iser, Wolfgang, "Interaction between Text and Reader." In *The Reader in the Text*, edited by Susan R. Suleiman and Inge Crossman. Princeton: Princeton University Press, 1980.

Jakobson, Roman. *Lingüística, poética, tiempo*. Barcelona: Editorial Crítica, 1981.

Jiménez, Juan Ramón. *Segunda antolojía poética*. Madrid: Espasa-Calpe, 1987.

Krieger, Murray. *Words about Words about Words*. Baltimore: Johns Hopkins University Press, 1988.

Kushigian, Julia. *Orientalism in the Hispanic Literary Tradition.* Albuquerque: University of New Mexico Press, 1991.

Lacan, Jacques. *Ecrits I.* Paris: Editions du Seuil, 1966.

Lotman, Jurii. *Analysis of the Poetic Text.* Ann Arbor, Mich.: Ardis, 1978.

Mallarmé, Stéphane. *Oeuvres completes.* Paris: Gallimard, 1945.

Mayhew, Jonathan. *Claudio Rodríguez and the Language of Poetic Vision.* Lewisburg, Pa.: Bucknell University Press, 1990.

Nealon, Jeffrey T., "The Discipline of Deconstruction." *PMLA* 107, no. 5 (October 1992): 1266–79.

Norris, Christopher. *Deconstruction: Theory and Practice.* New York: Methuen, 1982.

———. *What's Wrong with Postmodernism.* Baltimore: Johns Hopkins University Press, 1991.

Perloff, Marjorie. *The Poetics of Indeterminacy.* Princeton: Princeton University Press, 1981.

Riffaterre, Michael. *Semiotics of Poetry.* Bloomington: University of Indiana Press, 1978.

Rigolot, François. "Le poétique et l'analogique." In *Sémantique de la poésie,* edited by T. Todorov et al. Paris: Editions du Seuil, 1979.

Robbe-Grillet, Alain. *For a New Novel.* Translated by Richard Howard. New York: Grove Press, 1965.

Running, Thorpe. "Responses to the Politics of Oppression by Poets in Argentina and Chile." *Hispania,* Vol 73, No. 1 (March 1990): 40–49.

Sucre, Guillermo. *La máscara, la transparencia.* Mexico City: Fondo de Cultura Económica, 1985.

Vallejo, César. *Obra poética.* Critical edition coordinated by Américo Ferrari. Paris: Archivos, 1988.

———. *Poesía completa.* Mexico City: Premiá Editora, 1983.

Works by and about the Poets

JORGE LUIS BORGES
Books of Poetry

La cifra. Madrid: Alianza Tres, 1981.

Los conjurados. Madrid: Alianza Editorial, 1985.

Obra poética (1923–1977). Buenos Aires: Emecé, 1977.

El otro, el mismo. Buenos Aires: Emecé, 1969.

Critical Studies

Collin, Françoise. "From Blanchot to Borges." In *Borges and His Successors,* edited by Edna Aizenberg. Columbia: University of Missouri Press, 1990.

Echavarría, Arturo. *Lengua y literatura de Borges.* Barcelona: Editorial Ariel, 1983.

Molloy, Sylvia. "'Dios acecha en los intervalos': simulacro y causalidad textual en la ficción de Borges." *Revista Iberoamericana* 100–101 (July-December 1977): 381–98.

———. *Signs of Borges.* Translated by Oscar Montero and Sylvia Molloy. Durham, N.C.: Duke University Press, 1994.

Rodríguez Monegal, Emir. "Borges y la 'nouvelle critique.'" In *Jorge Luis Borges,* edited by Jaime Alazraki. Madrid: Taurus, 1976.

———. "Borges and Derrida Apothecaries." In *Borges and His Successors,* edited by Edna Aizenberg. Columbia: University of Missouri Press, 1990.

ALBERTO GIRRI
Books of Poetry

Existenciales. Buenos Aires: Editorial Sudamericana, 1986.

Monodias. Buenos Aires: Editorial Sudamericana, 1985.

Páginas de Alberto Girri. Buenos Aires: Editorial Sudamericana, 1986.

Tramas de conflictos. Buenos Aires: Editorial Sudamericana, 1988.

Critical Studies

Pezzoni, Enrique. Interview with Girri. In *Obra poética* by Alberto Girri. Vol. 4, 145–65. Buenos Aires: Corregidor, 1984.

Slade Pascoe, Muriel. *La poesía de Alberto Girri.* Buenos Aires: Editorial Sudamericana, 1986.

DAVID HUERTA
Books of Poetry

Cuaderno de noviembre. Mexico City: Alacena/Era, 1976.

Incurable. Mexico City: Era, 1987.

El jardín de la luz. Mexico City: UNAM, 1972.

Versión. Mexico City: Fondo de Cultura Económica, 1978.

Critical Studies

Ahern, Maureen. "La poesía de David Huerta." *Eco* 255 (January 1983): 248–69.

Asiain, Aurelio. "*Incurable* de David Huerta." *Vuelta* 138 (May 1988): 50–53.

Barreda Villarreal, Raquel. "David Huerta." *Vogue* (Mexico City), November 1988, 189–90.

Reyes, Juan José. "David Huerta: curar las pasiones tristes." *El Semanario,* 11 October 1987, 5.

ROBERTO JUARROZ
Works of, or on, Poetry

"Aproximaciones a la poesía moderna." *El Jabalí,* no. 3 (1994): 4–14.

Novena poesía vertical y Décima poesía vertical. Buenos Aires: Carlos Lohlé, 1986.

Poesía vertical. Caracas: Monte Avila, 1976.

Poesía y creación: diálogos con Guillermo Boido. Buenos Aires: Carlos Lohlé, 1980.

Undécima poesía vertical. Valencia: Pre-textos, 1988.

Critical Studies

Marco, Joaquín. "*Poesía vertical. Antología.*" *ABC literario* 35 (10 July 1992): 8.

Rodríguez Padrón, Jorge. "La aventura poética de Roberto Juarroz." *Nueva Estafeta,* 54 (1983): 47–54.

JUAN LUIS MARTÍNEZ
Poetry

La nueva novela. Santiago: Ediciones Archivo, 1985. Facsimile edition of the first edition of 1977.

"From *The New Novel.*" Translated and with an introduction by Jack Schmitt. *Review,* no. 49 (Fall 1994): 71–83.

Critical Studies

Daydí-Tolson, Santiago. "La obra de Juan Luis Martínez: un ejemplo de poética chilena actual." *Romance Languages Annual* 3 (1991): 406–10.

Lihn, Enrique, and Pedro Lastra. *Señales de ruta de Juan Luis Martínez.* Santiago de Chile: Ediciones Archivo, 1987.

Roblero Cum, María Ester. "Juan Luis Martínez: 'Me complace irradiar una identidad velada.'" *El Mercurio,* no. 202 (14 March 1993): 1, 4–5.

Valdivieso, Jaime. "El contra-universo entre las páginas de un libro." *La Época,* 11 September 1988, 3.

GONZALO MILLÁN
Books of Poetry

La ciudad. Ottawa: Les Editions Maison Culturelle Québec-Amérique Latine, 1979.

"Hacia la objetividad." In *Entre la lluvia y el arcoiris (Antología de jóvenes poetas chilenos),* edited by Soledad Bianchi. Rotterdam: Ediciones del Instituto para el Nuevo Chile, 1983.

Relación personal. Santiago: Arancibia Hermanos, 1968.

Virus. Santiago: Ediciones Ganymedes, 1987.

Critical Studies

Foxley, Carmen, and Ana María Cúneo. *Seis poetas de los sesenta.* Santiago de Chile: Editorial Universitaria, 1991.

Freidemberg, Daniel. "Gonzalo Millán." *Diario de la Poesía,* Winter 1991, 28–29.

OCTAVIO PAZ
Works of, or on, Poetry

Alternating Current. Translated by Helen R. Lane. New York: Viking, 1973.

Arbol adentro. Barcelona: Seix Barral, 1987.

The Bow and the Lyre. Translated by Ruth L. C. Simms. Austin: University of Texas Press, 1973.

Conjunctions and Disjunctions. Translated by Helen R. Lane. New York: Viking, 1974.

Libertad bajo palabra. Mexico City: Fondo de Cultura Económica, 1960.

Los hijos del limo. Barcelona: Seix Barral, 1974.

Pasado en claro. Mexico City: Fondo de Cultura Económica, 1978.

Salamandra. Mexico City: Joaquín Mortiz, 1962.

Los signos en rotación y otros ensayos. Madrid: Alianza Editorial.

Critical Studies

Durán, Manuel. "La huella del Oriente en la poesía de Octavio Paz." In *Octavio Paz,* edited by Pere Gimferrer. Madrid: Taurus, 1982.

Madrid, Lelia. "Octavio Paz: la invención del origen." *Insula* 46, no. 532–35 (April-May 1991): 27–28.

Oviedo, José Miguel. "Los pasos de la memoria." *Revista de Occidente* 14 (1976): 42-44, 51.

Pizarnik, Alejandra. "El premio internacional de poesía: *Salamandra.*" In *Octavio Paz,* edited by Pere Gimferrer. Madrid: Taurus, 1982.

Ruiz Barrionuevo, Carmen. "La incesante búsqueda del lenguaje en la poesía de Octavio Paz." *Revista de Filología de la Universidad de La Laguna* 3 (1984): 61–84.

Wilson, Jason. *Octavio Paz: A Study of His Poetics.* London: Cambridge University Press, 1979.

Yurkiévich, Saúl. "Octavio Paz, indagador de la palabra." In *Octavio Paz,* edited by Pere Gimferrer. Madrid: Taurus, 1982.

ALEJANDRA PIZARNIK

Books of Poetry

El deseo de la palabra. Barcelona: Ocnos, 1975.

"El poeta y su poema." In *Antología consultada de la joven poesía argentina.* Buenos Aires: Fabril Editora, 1968.

Obras completas. Buenos Aires: Corregidor, 1991.

La última inocencia y Las aventuras perdidas. Buenos Aires: Botella al mar, 1976.

Critical Studies

Caulfield, Carlota. "Entre la poesía y la pintura: elementos surrealistas en *Extracción de la piedra de locura* y *El infierno musical* de Alejandra Pizarnik." *Chasqui* 21, no. 1 (May 1992): 3–10.

Malinow, Inés. "Juicios críticos." In *Poesía argentina contemporánea.* Buenos Aires: Fundación Argentina para la Poesía, 1980.

Schwartz, Perla. *El quebranto del silencio: mujeres suicidas del siglo XX* Mexico City: Editorial Diana, 1989.

Index

Ahern, Maureen, 187 n. 2
Apollinaire, Guillaume, 17
Arenas, Braulio, 30
Arnheim, Rudolf, 73, 183 n. 2, 184 n. 4
Asiain, Aurelio, 187 n. 18

Barreda Villarreal, Raquel, 187 n. 3
Barry, Kevin, 74, 184 n. 6
Barthes, Roland, 158
Beckett, Samuel, 165
Blanchot, Maurice, 52, 55, 57–58, 65, 69, 99–102, 125, 165, 183 nn. 6 and 10, 185 nn. 12, 14, 16, and 17
Bly, Robert, 162
Boido, Guillermo, 51
Booth, Wayne, 78
Borges, Jorge Luis, 18, 52, 118, 124–39, 145, 167, 169
Breton, André, 30–33, 45
Bruns, Gerald, 14–17, 181 n. 2
Burroughs, William S., 146

Caulfield, Carlota, 184 n. 4
Cocteau, Jean, 97
Cohn, Robert Greer, 18–19, 181 n. 10
Collin, Françoise, 136–37, 185 n. 13
Costa, René de, 28–29, 182 n. 24
Cortázar, Julio, 75
Culler, Jonathan, 100, 185 n. 13

Darío, Rubén, 25, 86, 164
Daydí-Tolson, Santiago, 73–74, 183 n. 3, 184 n. 7
de Man, Paul, 19, 181 n. 9
Derrida, Jacques, 16–18, 52–58, 60, 65, 71–72, 125–27, 146–47, 151, 154, 157, 159, 162, 167, 170, 181 n. 9, 183 nn. 4 and 7, 186 nn. 6 and 7, 187 nn. 8, 9, and 17
Diego, Gerardo, 24–25
Donne, John, 13
Duchamp, Marcel, 82, 180

Durán, Manuel, 40, 183 n. 10

Echavarría, Arturo, 125, 185 n. 2
Eliot, T. S., 105, 109

Felman, Shoshana, 187 nn. 10 and 12
Foucault, Michel, 40, 125
Foxley, Carmen, 140, 186 nn. 4, 5 and 7
Franco, Jean, 26, 182 n. 18
Freidemberg, Daniel, 139, 186 n. 2
Fuertes, Gloria, 22

Genette, Gérard, 125
Girri, Alberto, 105–24, 153
Góngora y Argote, Luis de, 13, 14, 15
Greimas, A. J., 128
Guillén, Jorge, 167
Gutiérrez Nájera, Manuel, 163–64

Huerta, David, 24, 153–77, 179–80
Huerta, Efraín, 154
Huidobro, Vicente, 17, 24, 25, 27–30, 179

Iser, Wolfgang, 75, 78, 184 n. 9

Jakobson, Roman, 46, 50, 109, 128, 186 n. 9
Jiménez, Juan Ramón, 22–24
Juarroz, Roberto, 21, 24, 26–27, 51–72, 81, 86, 89, 106, 128–29, 177–80

Kierkegaard, Søren, 67
Krieger, Murray, 106, 108, 115, 118, 123, 185 nn. 4, 5, 7, and 11
Kushigian, Julia, 183 n. 12

Lacan, Jacques, 43, 128, 154, 157–59, 161–62, 187 nn. 11 and 12
Laforgue, Jules, 25
Lastra, Pedro, 74, 81, 184 nn. 5 and 14

193